W9-CDV-085

Main   Dec 2016

This item no longer belongs to Davenport Public Library

DAVENPORT PUBLIC LIBRARY
321 MAIN STREET
DAVENPORT, IOWA 52801-1490

Megan Dowd Lambert
in association with **The Eric Carle Museum of Picture Book Art**

Reading Picture Books ~~to~~ with Children

HOW TO SHAKE UP STORYTIME AND GET KIDS TALKING ABOUT WHAT THEY SEE

(TITLE PAGE)

endpaper

Foreword by **Chris Raschka**

 **Charlesbridge**

To Anna Markus

dedication

Text copyright © 2015 by Megan Dowd Lambert
Cover illustration copyright © 2015 by Laura Vaccaro Seeger
Interior image credits located on page 143

Smyth-sewn bind

All rights reserved, including the right of reproduction in whole or in part in any form.
Charlesbridge and colophon are registered trademarks of Charlesbridge Publishing, Inc.

metatextual content

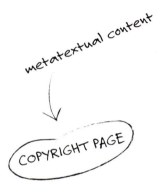
COPYRIGHT PAGE

Published by Charlesbridge
85 Main Street
Watertown, MA 02472
(617) 926-0329
www.charlesbridge.com

Library of Congress Cataloging-in-Publication Data
Lambert, Megan Dowd.
Reading picture books with children: how to shake up storytime and get kids
talking about what they see/Megan Dowd Lambert in association with the
Eric Carle Museum of Picture Book Art.
pages cm
Includes index.
ISBN 978-1-58089-662-7 (reinforced for library use)
ISBN 978-1-60734-563-3 (ebook)
ISBN 978-1-60734-695-1 (ebook pdf)
1. Picture books for children—Educational aspects.
2. School children—Books and reading.
3. Language arts. 4. Storytelling. I. Title.
LB1044.9.P49L36 2015
372.133—dc23
2014010501

Printed in China
(hc) 10 9 8 7 6 5 4 3 2 1

Display type set in the Museo family, designed by Jos Buivenga for exljbris
Text type set in Adobe Garamond
Printed and bound by 1010 Printing International Limited in Huizhou, Guangdong, China
Production supervision by Brian G. Walker
Designed by Susan Mallory Sherman

Table of Contents

front matter {

Foreword v

Preface • **Reading ~~to~~ *with* Children** vii

Introduction • **How I Learned to Think with My Eyes** xiii

Chapter 1 • **That's About the Size of It**

Trim Size and Orientation 3

Chapter 2 • **Coming Attractions**

Jackets and Covers 15

Chapter 3 • **Visual Overtures**

Endpapers 25

Chapter 4 • **Slow Down and Look**

Front Matter 31

Chapter 5 • **Knocked Out by Type**

Typography 38

Chapter 6 • **Gutter Talk and More**

Page Design 51

Chapter 7 • **"Children, Children, What Do You See?"**
Nurturing Visual Intelligence..66

Chapter 8 • **The Picture Book Playground**
The Benefits (and Fun) of the Whole Book Approach...................81

Conclusion • **The Story Continues**......................................95

Acknowledgments..103
Resources...108
    Leading Whole Book Approach Storytimes........................108
    Whole Book Approach Sample Questions..........................116
    Glossary of Book and Storytime Terminology...................129
    Further Reading..134
Notes..138
Image Credits...143
Index..146

back matter

gutter

Foreword

Why do we love books so much? Why do some of us, when we're children, drag around picture books just like stuffed animals? I had a brown monkey—straw-filled—whose hands and feet were many times mended and finally completely re-sewn by my mother. And I had *Die fröhlichen Steinzeitkinder* (*The Stone Age Children*) and *Die Steinzeit-kinder in Ägypten* (*The Stone Age Children in Egypt*) by Bertil Almqvist (published originally in Swedish). All three objects were essential to my young well-being.

The monkey is gone—I don't remember when he was lost—but the two books by Mr. Almqvist still stand on my shelves in remarkably good shape. They are the most tangible connection to my childhood self that I have.

Books, like stuffed animals, are things. They're very thingy. They have a size and a shape. They are more or less shiny, soft or hard, smooth or rough. The paper within them is glossy or matte, brilliant or warm, exciting or comforting.

Megan Dowd Lambert shows us how valuable all this thinginess of books is for students, teachers, and parents.

v

trim size

7 3/8"   9"

There is a fundamental joy in it. In the classroom and in our homes a picture book is one corner of the triangle completed by the teacher (or parent, or sibling, or friend) and the child. Each is essential. A horror (to my mind) of a modern classroom is the illuminated SMART board in a darkened room. The Very Hungry Caterpillar may look marvelous and big and glowing, but two necessary elements of good education are quite literally left in the dark: the teacher and the student. Learning is best when it comes with a personality, whether that personality is in the line of a brush, the smile of a teacher, or the question of a child.

One way to judge the merit of a work of art is to ask whether it grows more beautiful as it grows older. *Reading Picture Books with Children* begins by looking at Ludwig Bemelmans's *Madeline*. I remember my first reaction to this book: I was thrilled by that loose-painted line, by the simplicity and perfection of the drawing of Madeline herself, and by the wit of the poetry. The line, the drawing, and the poetry have only increased in beauty for me since then.

And this idea of beauty growing over time can be true of the book, the thing itself, too. As an author, to be handed one of my own books that has been torn and taped, smudged and erased, bent and smoothed, the four corners of the cardboard cover separating like little paper pussy willows, is one of my greatest satisfactions. There, in my hand, is the story around the story, the tale of a book that has traveled from hand to hand, mind to mind, heart to heart.

—*Chris Raschka*

Reading ~~to~~ *with* Children

I n 2001 I was a graduate student studying children's literature at Simmons College, and I heard that a new museum devoted to picture book art was slated to open a year later in Amherst, Massachusetts, right in my backyard. After some finagling, I managed to earn the final four credits toward my master's degree through an independent study in which I documented my work on behalf of the burgeoning education department of the Eric Carle Museum of Picture Book Art. The museum was founded by the artist Eric Carle and his wife, Barbara, and remains the only full-scale museum in the United States focused on picture books and their art form. (For more information see the Carle's website: www.carlemuseum.org.) By the time the Carle's grand opening occurred on November 22, 2002, I'd laid the groundwork for the Whole Book Approach, a co-constructive (interactive) storytime model centered on the picture book as a visual art form, which I'd used with

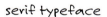

serif typeface

more than eight thousand children across Massachusetts in anticipation of that day.

Fast-forward eight years, and I'd worked with more than twenty-five thousand students and about three thousand professionals by leading hundreds of Whole Book Approach storytimes and professional development programs for the Carle. Meanwhile, I was also teaching at Simmons and other schools, raising my growing family, serving on book award committees, and making forays into speaking and writing about picture books and my experiences reading them with children. The confluence of my family life as the mother of five children and my professional life in children's literature all felt pretty happily-ever-after, but as I shifted into full-time teaching at Simmons and less programming work at the Carle, I knew I wanted to round out my work on the Whole Book Approach with a book—with *this* book.

The Eric Carle Museum of Picture Book Art

I set out to document what the Whole Book Approach is, how I developed it, how I've seen it work, and how I hope others will be able to use its techniques for understanding, reading, and sharing the picture book as a visual art form. I also wanted my book to tell the stories that have resulted from my purposeful decision to "shake up storytime" and use the Whole Book Approach to actively invite kids to talk about what they see. The stories are just too good to keep to myself. Besides, amid what can seem like a chorus of voices tying shared reading to test scores, or linking certain titles to certain curricular objectives, or succumbing to a descent into some fuzzy platitudes about "the magic of reading," I wanted to reflect on and value specific moments of insight, delight, wonder, puzzlement, and pleasure that have arisen from the times when I've met children in the pages of picture books and have really listened to what they have to say about what they see and hear.

I started working toward these goals with support from Mass Literacy, which named me a 2009 Massachusetts Literacy Champion. This award provided funding to support my work reviewing pieces I'd previously written about my development of the Whole Book Approach. I then embarked on the process of writing, revising, and researching an early version of this

> **The Whole Book Approach . . . is at its essence a means of reading picture books *with* children, as opposed to reading *to* them.**

pull quote

book, while also compiling permissions contacts for a manuscript proposal. The Carle was supportive of my efforts—staff members nominated me for the award, provided early editorial support, and acted as both sounding boards and advocates as I started shopping the work-in-progress to various publishing houses. When Charlesbridge emerged as the ideal publisher, we were all excited to proceed.

The result is this overview of the Whole Book Approach,

which is at its essence a means of reading picture books *with* children, as opposed to reading *to* them. During Whole Book Approach storytimes, children's active participation in making meaning of all they see and hear during a picture book reading takes precedence over moving through the pages at the pace of the adult's oral reading of the text. The word "approach" is crucial—this is not a prescriptive method that would have you asking specific questions about picture book illustration and design in a certain order as you read aloud. Instead, the Whole Book Approach simply stresses inviting children to react to the *whole* book—its art, design, production, paratextual and textual elements—in ways that feel natural and enriching to them and to you as the adult reader. This method requires that storytime leaders—be they teachers, librarians, parents, or other adults engaged in reading picture books with children—immerse themselves in understanding the picture book as a multimodal art form (one that uses both visual and verbal modes of communication) in order to consider how not only text and illustration but *all* design and production elements might contribute to the shared reading.

Such work seems all the more exciting amid ebook developments and other technological advances. Even as books leave the page and take root on the screens of myriad reading devices, I'm convinced that the simple codex design (separate sheets bound together at one side with a cover) of the objects we call books has staying power, particularly when it comes to shared reading transactions of

fac

the sort that picture books invite, and I acknowledge a mixture of sentimentality and practicality in this statement. I found kinship in this position at the 2013 Horn Book at Simmons Colloquium, where I listened to Boston Globe–Horn Book Award judge Sarah Ellis remark that in her review of what seemed like an abundance of books about books, she'd noticed "a huge and possibly slightly melancholy affection for the printed book" amid the changes to publishing and reading in the digital age. Then Ellis went on to say, "What all these books reminded me of was the immense flexibility of the printed book as a medium . . . [and] we still seem to be testing those limits."[1]

es

Although Ellis was talking about artists, writers, and publishers testing the limits of the codex design, Whole Book Approach storytimes help children test these limits, too, by supporting their development into readers who are fully engaged with the physical, material codex picture book. This work anticipates, not the death of the book in the digital age, but rather rich opportunity for books that make the most of what might be called their bookness. Film critic James Monaco refers to this materiality of the book as "the 'thing-ness of a book,'"[2] while children's literature scholar Aidan Chambers refers to "the book-as-object," continuing on to say that a book:

is a piece of sculpture which, like any piece of sculpture, can please or displease us, cause us to make this or that association. And this book-sculpture not only has shape and weight and texture as well as visual appeal, it also

extracted quote

has a smell and is mobile—it can be open and closed
(with more or less satisfaction in the way it does this)
and be carried easily about with us.[3]

As a reader, a mother, and a teacher, I know that we carry picture books about with us, not just as physical objects in our hands with pages that we turn, but as remembered experiences with stories and art, and with each other. I pick up a single picture book, and I recall not only the specific story and art on its pages but also the myriad insights that it provoked through Whole Book Approach readings that invited children to read words, pictures, and design along with me.

"But doesn't interrupting the reading to talk about art and design undermine getting lost in a story?"

"How do you keep it from devolving into chaos?"

"Co-constructive? Para-whats?"

As you read on to discover answers to these questions and to others that this preface may have provoked, my hope is that you'll have even *more* questions and ideas as you reflect on how you might use the Whole Book Approach to shake up your storytimes, too.

—Megan Dowd Lambert
Amherst, MA

VERSO PAGE

How I Learned to Think with My Eyes

When I enrolled in my first graduate courses at Simmons College, I imagined myself reconnecting with novels I'd loved as a child, as well as discovering new favorites—and learning new ways of thinking about all of them. I planned on getting up close and personal with the likes of Anne, Laura, Caddie, Cassie, Jo, Ramona, Dicey, and Harriet, and I couldn't wait. I didn't really know what I was going to do with the degree, but I knew it was the field I

Simmons College

wanted to enter. So in the fall of 2000, I dutifully registered for a required literary theory course, an elective on folk and fairy tales, and finally, another required course on picture books. As we reviewed the syllabus for the picture book course on the first day, I had a revelation.

Picture books.

Picture. Books.

I was going to have to think about pictures.

About art.

About design (whatever that was).

I was (and am) a word lover. A sucker for a good story. A shameless practitioner of marginalia. A devotee of character, voice, theme, and (to some extent) plot. And, most especially, a compulsive re-reader who thinks that criticism doesn't pull books apart so much as it opens them up to a multiplicity of possible meanings. I learn best through my ears and am a big talker, too. Lo and behold, this predilection for words and text had made me overlook the word "picture" in the course title, in the very name of the form, and I'd walked into class expecting to be reading and talking and writing about authors and texts, story themes, and implied audience, with perhaps a nod to how cute or lovely the illustrations were. Just reading the titles of the articles and critical texts listed on the syllabus showed me how very misguided I'd been:

Picture This: How Pictures Work by Molly Bang
Myth, Magic, and Mystery: One Hundred Years of American Children's Book Illustration by Michael Patrick Hearn, Trinkett Clark, and H. Nichols B. Clark
Looking at Pictures in Picture Books by Jane Doonan
"Introduction to Picturebook Codes" by William Moebius

And on, and on . . .

Introduction

What was I going to do in a class that was pretty much all about art and design?

"I've never really studied art," I sheepishly told Susan Bloom, co-instructor of the course and director of the program at that time.

"Well," she said brightly, "now's your chance!"

It's not as though I grew up in a cultural vacuum without art. Both of my siblings are artists. The elementary school we attended had art-appreciation courses in addition to regular art classes. We took regular field trips to the magnificent Sterling and Francine Clark Art Institute in Williamstown, Massachusetts, and I'd visited art museums now and again throughout my life. But art just wasn't my thing. Or so I thought. The picture book class showed me that actually, art *could* be my thing—even if I wasn't an artist. I'd just have to learn to think with my eyes.

Once I'd recognized the picture book as a multimodal form, I started to think visually by embracing what nineteenth-century illustrator Walter Crane had to say about the "architectural plan"[4] of the book. Michael Patrick Hearn, co-instructor of the picture book course with Susan Bloom, lectured extensively on Crane as the father of the picture book form, drawing upon *Of the Decorative Illustration of Books Old and New*, in which Crane writes:

> *A book may be the home of both thought and vision. Speaking figuratively, in regard to book decoration, some*

knockout type

Art *could* be my thing—even if I wasn't an artist. I'd just have to learn to think with my eyes.

are content with a rough shanty in the woods, and care only to get as close to nature in her most superficial aspects as they can. Others would surround their house with a garden indeed, but they demand something like an architectural plan. They would look at a frontispiece like a façade; they would take hospitable encouragement from the title-page as from a friendly inscription over the porch; they would hang a votive wreath at the dedication, and so pass on into the hall of welcome, take the author by the hand and be led by him and his artist from room to room, as page after page is turned, fairly decked and adorned with picture and ornament and device.[5]

Part of the reason Crane's figurative words resonated so powerfully with me is that I love a good metaphor, and similes make me smile; reading Crane's likening of a picture book to a house unshuttered my eyes to the picture book as a visual art form. As much as I still wanted to sink my critical teeth into novels such as *Little House on the Prairie*, I quickly realized that I was no longer "content with a rough shanty" of a picture book. I wanted to learn all I could about picture book art and design—about the architecture of the book. After hearing my instructor read those words, I wanted to face the "frontispiece like a façade." I longed to "take hospitable encouragement from the title-page as from a friendly inscription over the porch." I committed to noting the dedication page's role as "votive wreath" to the book proper. This notion was exciting but also a bit daunting, since engaging critically with art and design was all new to me. The architecture of the book had become my academic home, and although I wasn't quite sure how I'd settle into it with my particular background and lack of formal artistic study, I walked right inside and sat down to feast my eyes on all the picture book had to offer.

About a year later, in the summer of 2001, I was four credits shy of completing my degree. I'd spent the prior academic year traveling back and forth between my home in western Massachusetts and Simmons's campus in Boston to take classes. Although it tickled me that the bus line I used for traveling across the state was named for Peter Pan, and although I'd put those many hours on the turnpike to good use by completing course readings, I wanted to pursue an independent study closer to home to round out my degree and launch me onto a career path.

The Eric Carle Museum of Picture Book Art was still more than a year away from its grand opening in Amherst, Massachusetts, but when I heard that the Carle had an information office close to my home in Northampton, I was intrigued. I took my then four-year-old son, Rory, to the office's weekly, volunteer-led storytime and decided to throw my hat in the ring to see how I could help the Carle while pursuing my academic and professional goals. Founding director Nick Clark (co-author, as H. Nichols B. Clark, of the picture book course's text *Myth, Magic, and Mystery*) offered me several possibilities: leading the weekly storytime in the office, compiling a bibliography to inform purchasing decisions for the Carle's future reading library, conducting interviews with teachers and librarians throughout the region to see how the Carle might partner with them and support their work, and leading visiting storytimes in schools and libraries as thanks for their staffs' participation in the interviews. Taking my cue from a certain Very Busy Spider, I decided to tackle all these projects and to document the work, not only to finish up my degree but also to launch a not-so-covert effort to make myself indispensable to what I already knew would be a remarkable place.

I started off leading traditional storytimes of the sort I'd led as a volunteer in my son's preschool and in the public library where I worked part-time: I chose a theme to link the books, songs, finger play, and craft activity I'd planned for the day. Children sat and listened to the books and engaged in the other activities, and then we talked about the books when we were done reading them. It was all quite fun.

But as I set up my schedule for the visiting storytimes in regional schools and libraries, I started thinking more intentionally about the fact that I was representing an art museum, and I stopped and wondered why I was bothering to structure storytimes around snow, or bunnies, or planes, or giraffes, or whatever theme I'd chosen. I thought about shifting from structuring storytime in a way that forced thematic connections between books and instead began envisioning an approach that would invite children to engage with great picture book art on their own terms.

> **I . . . began envisioning an approach that would invite children to engage with great picture book art on their own terms.**

I took much inspiration from Abigail Housen and

Introduction

Philip Yenawine's Visual Thinking Strategies (VTS), an inquiry-based approach to looking at art that the Carle planned to implement in its galleries. VTS turns the traditional museum docent tour on its head by having the group leader ask visitors open-ended questions about the art on the wall instead of telling the group about the art they are viewing: "What's going on in this picture? What do you see that makes you say that? What more can we find?"[6] The ensuing discussions last about twenty minutes per picture, and there is compelling documentation of the approach's success in fostering not only engagement with art in the moment but also critical-thinking skills that last well beyond the discussion.

> **What's going on in this picture?**
> **What do you see that makes you say that?**
> **What more can we find?**

How could I adapt this approach to picture book readings? I knew that I couldn't, shouldn't, and wouldn't lead twenty-minute VTS discussions on every page of a picture book. That would be deadly. But I could take the inquiry-based essence of VTS and shift from what literacy experts call "performance story times"[7] to leading "co-constructive"[8] storytimes. In the performance approach, the children and teacher engage in conversation mostly *before* and *after* the reading, while in the co-constructive approach, there is a large amount of talk *during* the reading of the book. In the 1990s, Grover J. "Russ" Whitehurst (now the Director of the Brown Center on Education Policy and an expert on reading, teacher quality, student assessment, learning and instruction, education technology, and pre-school programs) developed a co-constructive model that he called dialogic reading, in which the adult reader asks a prescribed series of open-ended questions, engages children in interactive conversations about the book, and expands on children's comments. Its central technique is called the PEER sequence, in which the adult takes the following steps: **P**rompts the child to say something about the book; **E**valuates the child's response; **E**xpands the child's response by rephrasing and adding information to it; and **R**epeats the prompt to make sure the child has learned from the expansion.[9] Studies have found that this approach substantially improves young children's emergent literacy skills and expressive vocabulary after only a few sessions.[10]

Indeed, the Public Library Association and the Association for Library Service to Children adopted dialogic reading as the foundation of their joint Every Child Ready to Read initiative, launched in 2001. As I learned more about VTS and dialogic reading, I was heartened by the research-based evidence that supported stopping and talking about a book *during* a reading as a way of enhancing comprehension, engagement, vocabulary acquisition, and literacy skills. Meanwhile, as I worked to develop my own co-constructive model, I was mindful of my goal of engaging children with the whole book: its text-based story, yes, but also its visual elements—its art and design, its Walter Cranian architecture.

Not only did this focus on the visual make sense for my work on behalf of an art museum, it was also consistent with what had most excited me in my own study of the picture book at Simmons. Why shouldn't children be af-forded the same opportunity as adults for critical engage-ment with the picture book as a visual art form? Whereas di-alogic reading is often referred

> **I began to craft the Whole Book Approach as what might be described as "see, hear, and say reading."**

to as "hear and say reading,"[11] reflecting the fact that chil-dren hear something read aloud or hear a related question and say something in response, I began to craft the Whole Book Approach as what might be described as "*see*, hear, and say reading," by intentionally placing the emphasis of my questions and prompts on the illustration, design, and production elements of the picture book as an art form.

Furthermore, the focus of the burgeoning Whole Book Approach on the visual and physical elements of the picture book form also seemed to make good develop-mental sense. After all, we've all seen babies, toddlers, preschoolers, and emergent readers flip through the pages of a picture book and "read" it by examining pictures and design, so why not bring some of this early childhood "reading" right into story-time? And so, after leading one of my last themed story-times while dressed as a jack-o-lantern on Halloween, I

Megan Dowd Lambert and her son Stevie

turned my attention away from leading programs that were about particular holidays, animals, or other themes, and instead focused on making storytimes about the children who attended them.

This shifted focus, in turn, brought us deeply into the books we read together, proving the old adage that pictures are worth (at least) a thousand words—and the other one about kids saying the darndest things. When I started leading workshops on the Whole Book Approach at the Carle, teachers and librarians who were picture book aficionados and seasoned storytime leaders were delighted to have new ideas to incorporate into their work and told me time and again that the Whole Book Approach was a whole lot of fun, but also a whole lot more. I knew just what they meant: leading storytimes with this approach and intentionally allowing it to inform my reading at home with my own children ultimately enriched not just their experiences with picture books but my own as well. Storytimes became conversation times, and children made me see things I never would have discovered on my own as they brought questions and ideas to bear upon the picture books we read together—the *whole* books, including the paratexts.

Although he was not specifically referring to picture books, in his foreword to Gérard Genette's *Paratexts: Thresholds of Interpretation*, Richard Macksey lists specific parts of the book as he introduces Genette's examination of "the frame containing both the text itself and all the liminal devices—titles, signs of authorship, dedications, epigraphs, prefaces, notes, intertitles, epilogues, and the like—that mediate the relations between text and reader."[12] Genette's own titular adoption of the word "threshold" evokes, again, Walter Crane's notion of the architecture of the book. Since the multimodal picture book relies even more heavily on its visual elements and materiality than other types of books do, using the Whole Book Approach to invite children to notice the threshold before they enter the homey space of the book proper sets the stage for them to continue to make meaning of the visual elements of the picture book while its verbal text is read aloud. But in order to make the most of the interpretive possibilities provoked by this liminal space, the adult storytime leader needs to devote time to its consideration during a reading. The next chapters are devoted to supporting this consideration, deliberately ushering you, the reader of this book, across the paratextual thresholds of the picture book form and all it has to offer.

Reading Picture Books with to Children

HALF-TITLE PAGE

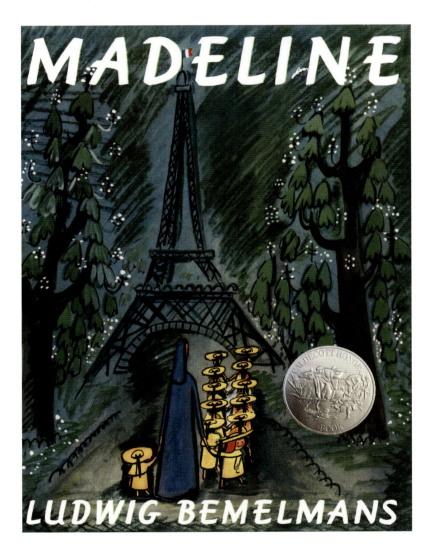

MADELINE

LUDWIG BEMELMANS

Chapter 1

That's About the Size of It

Trim Size and Orientation

chapter title

subtitle

"In an old house in Paris that was covered with vines, lived twelve little girls in two straight lines." When my children's literature professor at Smith College, Anna Markus, read these lines aloud one day, she let her voice trail off at the last clause so that the class could fill in the words. But I didn't know them! Somehow I'd missed out on Ludwig Bemelmans's classic *Madeline* as a child, but I immediately adored the title character—perhaps because she fit right in with all the feisty girls I loved in the novels I read, and even had red hair like Anne and Caddie. I've owned a copy of the book ever since; it's been a staple in my children's reading lives and pretend play (my younger son, Stevie, has often been dressed up like Madeline by his big sister Natayja), and it's a title I have returned to again and

3

folio (page number)

again as Whole Book Approach storytime fare, since it offers a great opportunity to make talking about book design a natural part of a reading.

Take a moment to think about the generous height of the hardcover edition of *Madeline*. Most picture books are rectangles, but they can adopt either a landscape (horizontal) or portrait (vertical) orientation, and the trim size (the final dimensions of the bound pages) varies dramatically from book to book. One notable feature of most picture books is that they are sized to comfortably accommodate a shared reading audience, as opposed to a solitary one. In *A Family of Readers*, Martha V. Parravano writes:

> *Consider a small child sitting on his mother's lap while she reads him a picture book. The picture book opens to a width that effectively places the child at the center of a closed circle—that of the mother's body, arms, and picture book. Or perhaps the child is too big or independent to sit on a parent's lap—he sits next to her, one person holding the left side of the picture book—the other the right side. Again a circle. I don't think it's an accident that so much adult-child book-sharing forms and takes place within a circle, or that so many picture books open to a size that facilitates one. That circle, so private and intimate, is a place apart from the demands and stresses of daily life, a sanctuary in and from which the child can explore the many worlds in picture books. Despite all of our society's technological*

advances, it still just takes one child, one book, and one reader to create this unique space, to work this everyday magic.[13]

Madeline's generous trim size and portrait orientation do comfortably accommodate a shared reading experience, but they do more than that, and in a Whole Book Approach storytime, I'm interested in inviting children to make meaning of *why* this book adopts such a tall portrait orientation, while others have different trim sizes and layouts. One day when I held the book up and asked a group of children to consider just this, a four-year-old regular attendee of storytime at the Carle looked at the cover art with those twelve little girls and the one, tall tower and exclaimed, "That book is so tall because of the"—he hesitated, trying to find the right words—"because of the . . . *heightful tower*!"

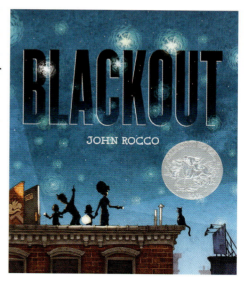

Indeed, Bemelmans's whimsical depictions of the Eiffel Tower and of Parisian cityscapes throughout the book demand a tall, portrait orientation, allowing the city to become as much a focus of the book as Madeline herself. Contemporary works such as John Rocco's *Blackout* also use the portrait layout to accommodate and embrace the height of buildings in urban landscapes, while Christopher Myers's *Wings* utilizes the height of the portrait trim size for thematic

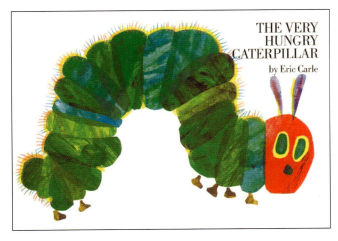

reasons—it tells the story of a city-dwelling boy who can fly. "The book goes up because Ikarus goes up to fly," commented a second grader during one reading.

Comparing and contrasting picture books with landscape and portrait orientations is something that I've invited even very young children to do with great success. They understand and articulate that in contrast with books like *Madeline*, *Blackout*, and *Wings*, Eric Carle's famed *The Very Hungry Caterpillar* adopts a landscape orientation because this shape best echoes the form of the caterpillar itself. Furthermore, the horizontal shape of the book bespeaks the page-to-page journey of the caterpillar as it makes its way through the foods lined up on successive pages. It's a small

leap for children to realize that most picture books about journeys adopt the landscape orientation because of the horizontal form's visual implication of movement through time and space in conjunction with the page turns. Think about the Polar Express going on its journey to the North Pole, or Peter walking through his

6

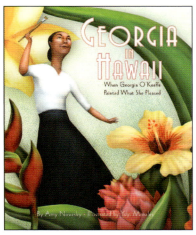

neighborhood on a snowy day, or Wanda Gág's "hundreds of cats, thousands of cats, millions and billions and trillions of cats" following the very old man home to the very old woman— just to name a few.

On the other hand, picture book biographies such as *Georgia in Hawaii: When Georgia Painted What She Pleased*, about the artist Georgia O'Keeffe and written by Amy Novesky with illustrations by Yuyi Morales, are often set in portrait layouts because the human form is vertical, and if the person profiled in the book is going to be the focus of many of the interior illustrations, it makes compositional sense for the book to adopt this vertical format. Picture book biographies such as *Ella Fitzgerald: The Tale of a Vocal Virtuosa* by Andrea Davis Pinkney and illustrated by Brian Pinkney, or *Moses: When Harriet Tubman Led Her People to Freedom* by Carole Boston Weatherford and illustrated by Kadir Nelson, and many, many others, affirm this design choice.

Perhaps this choice is most essential when a character's height is a defining attribute—see Julius Lester and Jerry Pinkney's *John Henry*, Anne Isaacs and Paul O.

> **Most picture books about journeys adopt the landscape orientation because of the horizontal form's visual implication of movement through time and space.**

Zelinsky's *Swamp Angel*, Kevin Hawkes' Wicked Big Toddlah picture books, or Steven Kellogg's *Paul Bunyan*. These are all examples of tall tales about tall characters that needed the books that feature them to be, well, tall.

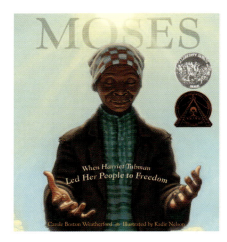

The portrait orientation is also used for other content-driven reasons. With its rebellion against gravity, the shape provides a logical physical space not only for books with urban settings, but also for those set in mountainous regions, such as Alice McLerran and Eric Carle's *The Mountain That Loved a Bird*. Contrast this with the landscape layout of Verna Aardema and Beatriz Vidal's *Bringing the Rain to Kapiti Plain*. This book, set in the Serengeti plains of Africa, demands a horizontal shape. Indeed, the paperback edition produced by Puffin Books for Reading Rainbow includes the cover art forced into a vertical orientation on the back of the book. Comparing the two pictures reveals how much is lost when the artwork is not allowed the horizontal space to depict the breadth of the expansive plains setting.

Although exceptional, other picture books adopt shaped formats—a term used to describe any book that is not a square or a rectangle. These are perhaps most common in board book editions, where a book about a bunny might be shaped like a bunny, perhaps to blur the line between toy and book for the babies reading the shaped books, or to physically underscore a key

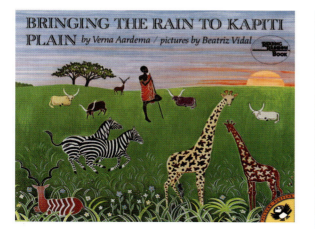

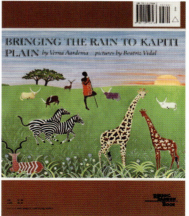

theme. (Of course, such a design also helps to make the book stand out among others on a shelf, which serves a marketing purpose.) There are some examples of shaped picture books, too—*Leonardo's Horse* by Jean Fritz and illustrated by Hudson Talbott is an excellent example. A starred review of the book from *Publishers Weekly* notes that the artist makes exceptional use of the shaped format: "a rectangle topped by a semi-circle: the rounded space by turns becomes a window through which da Vinci views a cloud shaped like a flying horse; the domed building that was Dent's studio and gallery; and a globe depicting the route the bronze horse travels on its way from the U.S. to Italy."[14]

Finally, a square trim size is sometimes used to support thematic elements of a given picture book. Michael

Hall's book *Perfect Square* sort of had to be, well, a perfect square. Although they're not quite equilateral, Laura Vaccaro Seeger's picture books *One Boy* and *First the Egg* have stories with circular resolutions that invite the visual symmetry of their nearly square shape. Furthermore, the square design can impart either a feeling of coziness or a

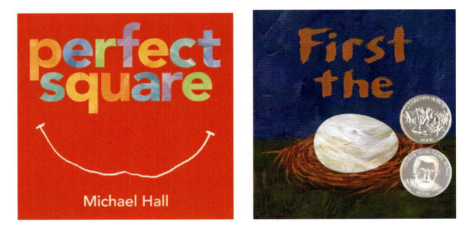

sense of claustrophobic entrapment, as four equal sides meet each other at four right corners. Molly Bang's delightfully creepy, wordless picture book *The Grey Lady and the Strawberry Snatcher* makes the most of its nearly square shape, which heightens the dramatic intensity of the chase scenes. In several page openings, full-bleed art (art that extends all the way to the edge of a page) might initially be read as a single, rectangular picture stretching out across the double-page spread. Closer inspection reveals two separate pictures confined to the facing verso (left-hand) page and recto (right-hand) page, with the gutter (the inner margin or seam where the pages are bound) of the book between them. This layout restricts the facing images to the nearly square format of the book instead of affording the art the expansiveness of the initially perceived full double-spread. The Grey Lady looks even more imperiled since she seems trapped on both the verso and recto. In stark contrast, Jonathan Bean's cozy little book *At Night*, with its small, nearly square trim size, imparts a feeling of security and calm with every page turn, as if the book itself were a goodnight hug to the reader.

Because the orientation or layout of a picture book is one of the most immediate elements of book design that readers notice, welcoming children to notice how layout choices inform their responses to picture books can feel rather like an intellectual hug, saying from the get-go that their perceptions matter in making meaning of the picture book form. This embracing of children's observations about the shape and orientation of a book extends into the related consideration of a picture book's dimensions, whether they are tiny and cozy like Bean's *At Night* or large and grand like *Madeline* with its "heightful tower." Oversized picture books like the "heightful" *Madeline* can create a dramatic stage for the visual story, and smaller books evoke a more intimate feeling for the reader. Beatrix Potter famously wanted to create "little books for little hands,"[15] and the small trim size of her books (4 by 5 ⅛ inches) lends an intimacy to the reading experience while also underscoring the small scale of the animals at the heart of her stories.

The picture book form is thus one area in which size

does matter. Perhaps there's no better example of this than the 2013 Boston Globe–Horn Book Honor book *Open This Little Book* by Jesse Klausmeier and illustrated by Suzy Lee. From the outside the book adopts a large portrait layout, rather than appearing to be the "little book" that the title suggests. But by following the title's directive, the reader discovers pages of diminishing trim sizes, books within books, nestled in one another. As reviewer Sarah

The picture book form is thus one area in which size does matter.

Ellis notes, "When we say a 'story within a story' we don't usually mean it this literally,"[16] but as this metafictive book draws attention to its very bookness through the various trim sizes housed within the boards of its generous portrait cover, readers gain a heightened awareness of their role in making meaning as they turn the shrinking and expanding pages and invest themselves in what they see.

"Hey, Mom-Mom!" my daughter Caroline excitedly said to me the first time we opened *Open This Little Book*. "We are *reading* about *reading*. Get it?"

And I did! But given how integral trim size is to a reader's experience of a picture book, one thing I have a hard time "getting" is book redesign that significantly alters trim size from one edition to another. While I can appreciate the desire that some hold for a larger copy of *The Tale of Peter Rabbit* to share with groups at storytimes, when the Carle hosted a Potter exhibition in 2005 and I used such an edition, I felt like I was looking at the art in a fun-house mirror. I often have similar concerns when I see "big books," which are designed to make it possible for large groups of children to see poster-sized picture books at storytime. Not only are these unwieldy for the adult reader trying to manage them and turn their pages (I've even seen people prop them up on easels), they also run the risk of undermining the aesthetic of the book as a whole.

On the other hand, when a picture book designed to be tall gets reprinted in a smaller size, sometimes the grandeur of the art is lost. A diminutive *Madeline*? To paraphrase Miss Clavel, "something is not right" about that. Indeed, one of the delights of picture books is that, like the characters who populate them, they come in a broad range of shapes and sizes. Scholar Leonard S. Marcus asked about this in an interview with illustrator Rosemary Wells:

> LSM: *The late 1960s and early 1970s was a time of small picture books. Besides your own, there were, for example, the very small books by Martha Alexander and Mercer Mayer. Did you enjoy working on that intimate scale? Why aren't more books like those being published now?*

> RW: *I still love little books. They're for little hands, and children love them, too. But now most books are large because publishers want a book to serve as a poster for itself. They want it seen across a big store. They want a book that is a big presence.*[17]

While "a big presence" may grab one's attention, sometimes good things come in small packages, as the old saying goes. That picture books can be big like Papa Bear, medium-sized like Mama Bear, or tiny like Baby Bear ensures that readers will find the one that's just right as they cozy up with their picture books, ready to make meaning of all the varied sizes and shapes the books can adopt.

Chapter 2

Coming Attractions

Jackets and Covers

While Walter Crane likened picture book design to architecture, many illustrators draw parallels between the picture book form and theater, essentially viewing the picture book as what artist Will Hillenbrand calls "the theater of the lap."[18] I like this, especially since the picture book has so much in common with film and theatrical plays: words and pictures work together to tell a story, to communicate, to provide information. Extending this analogy positions the book jacket as a coming-attraction poster hanging outside the theater, which invites readers to see the book jacket as a single entity, paying attention to its front and back sides, while also taking a look at any artwork on the interior jacket flaps.

Jacket art on picture books can adopt a wraparound design, with one picture extending from the front of the book across the spine to the back. When the back of the jacket reveals something surprising or illuminating, a wraparound design can create a dramatic moment for the viewer. For example, the wraparound jacket art for Emily Gravett's *Wolf Won't Bite!* shows three pigs on the front, with one of them holding a string that leads to the back of the book. Lo and behold, a shaggy-looking wolf is attached to that string, and though the pigs believe he "won't bite," he doesn't look happy to be there: intraiconic text (words that are an integral part of a picture) above him reads "Grrrr" in lettering made to look like his bristling gray fur. The implication is that despite what the title states, the wolf is not an entirely passive or complacent presence, which provokes curiosity in readers before the book begins—as long as they have a chance to look at both the front and the back of the jacket before the reading commences.

The practice of looking at the entirety of the jacket before reading a book during Whole Book Approach storytimes is something that grew out of my experiences reading at home with my sons and daughters. They like to examine the outside of the book before diving into its contents as a part of their selection process, and doing so often sparks recollections of past readings or insights into the art that guide and inform a current reading. For example, once, when reading Mo Willems and Jon J. Muth's *City Dog, Country Frog* at bedtime, we took the time to examine the jacket before reading the story, and they noticed a detail that had theretofore eluded me: surreptitiously situated on the slim spine of the picture book is Country Chipmunk, the character who makes a late entrance in the story, easing City Dog's loneliness after Country Frog has disappeared.

"If City Dog looked at that part of the book, he would

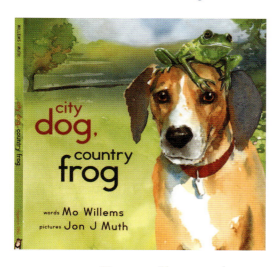

know he was going to have a new friend," my then five-year-old Caroline said.

The notion of the characters in a book existing outside the book charmed me, but I was also struck by how perceptive Caroline was about the book's design communicating something important to the reader: yes, the eponymous characters City Dog and Country Frog are the main focus of the story, but Country Chipmunk, with his cameo on the spine, ends up playing a crucial role in the story's resolution.

Such a fine detail might be difficult for a large group to examine, but dual-image jackets, their pictures divided into two scenes by the spine, can invite storytime attendees to make connections between front and back images. In Allen Say's *Grandfather's Journey*, the front of the jacket depicts a young man standing on the deck of a large ship. The back of the jacket has a small picture of an origami boat at its center.

As an exercise, think about the connections you can make between these two images. Or, put another way, how can you bring the pictures into dialogue with one another as you consider their juxtaposition on the book jacket? While this latter phrasing may seem more geared to an adult audience, children can certainly grapple with the impact of viewing full wraparound jacket art after viewing just the front image, or of making connections between front and back images. To support this inquiry, I often provoke children's engagement with a book at the beginning of a Whole Book Approach storytime by using the aforementioned open-ended questions gleaned from Visual Thinking Strategies: "What's going on in this picture? What do you see that makes you say that? What more can you find?" These questions invite children to make an emotional and cognitive investment in jacket art, provoking their curiosity about the book and encouraging them to continue reading pictures while I read the story aloud. When I've used these questions with *Grandfather's Journey*, many children have noted the dissonance between the titular word "grandfather" and the youthful figure on the front of the jacket.

"He's too young to be a grandfather," one child said.

"So maybe that's when Grandfather was little, and the book will be about his whole life," another offered.

And indeed it is: this book is about physical journeys across an ocean and throughout the United States, but it also tells the story of a temporal journey through Grandfather's lifetime as it details the emotional journey of the

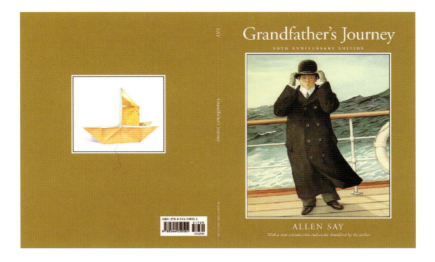

mostly offstage narrator (Allen Say himself) coming to understand and appreciate his grandfather and the similarities they share as people navigating a bicultural existence.

On this latter point, "Look how the front of the jacket has Grandfather on the ship in the Pacific Ocean," a second grader remarked after we had finished reading the book during an outreach visit I led in her classroom some years ago. "He really is between Japan and the US in that picture, and that's how he always feels even when he's not on the boat." This particularly astute, sensitive remark provoked a discussion in the class about immigration stories from the students' families, which led to the teacher creating a mini-unit about family journeys in order to embrace her students' investment in this theme.

Although conventional wisdom suggests that we shouldn't judge a book by its cover (or jacket), providing children with the time and space to reflect on jacket art can enhance their engagement with picture books at the start of a reading and give them rich opportunities to re-visit major themes, ideas, and questions at the end of a book. I'm particularly committed to *opening* storytime with questions instead of telling children what I think a book is about based on my own reading of the jacket art. My hope is that allowing them to steer the ship, so to speak, acknowledges that they are learning to read pictures as surely as they are learning to read words and invites them to express what they know and understand, not to mention what they are puzzled about, at the very begin-ning of a shared reading. Progressive educational ap-proaches posit active participation and the construction of one's own knowledge as the cornerstone of comprehension and retention in learning. This inquiry-driven reading of jacket art creates what Rosemary Agoglia, the founding curator of education at the Carle, called the "leaning-in effect," as children's attention is riveted at the outset of sto-rytime.

If reading jacket art produces this effect, removing the jacket to examine the picture book's casing heightens sto-rytime intrigue. There's something that seems slightly naughty about taking off a book jacket in a school or li-brary setting. (Though, of course, this isn't possible if the collection's processing procedure includes covering and taping down book jackets. If this is the case, one can usually still peek under the book jacket by lifting it up to see the cover boards underneath.)

> **I'm particularly committed to *opening* storytime with questions instead of telling children what I think a book is about.**

20

Although many hardcover books are bound with paper that simply replicates jacket art on the front and back boards of the cover, clothbound hardcover books often treat the viewer to the additional design element of debossed art, which can be colored with ink or foil or left as an unadorned impression on the casing in a process called blind stamping. At the very least, the book's design includes a chosen color for the clothbound casing, which often has a thematic or aesthetic connection to the jacket art.

While more expensive to produce, and therefore less common, clothbound casings are making a comeback, as evidenced by the following exchange between Leonard S. Marcus and editor Neal Porter:

> LSM: *I have heard a number of art directors say recently that they are putting more money into enhancing the production values of their traditional picture books with a view to highlighting the possibilities of the printed book.*
>
> NP: *I am doing that, too. For Julie Fogliano and Erin Stead's* If You Want to See a Whale, *I did a full cloth case with a "blind" stamp—an impressed image. The idea was to create a sort of sensory experience for the reader. It was the first cloth case I had done in twenty years!*[19]

The hue of the blue cloth binding of this picture book evokes the sea, and the simple blind stamp of the whale's form is like a promise to readers that they will indeed see a whale inside the pages of the picture book. During a dinner hosted by Macmillan (the parent company of the Neal Porter Books imprint) at the American Library Association's annual conference in 2013, Erin Stead offered a reason beyond the aesthetic for wanting a simple, cloth binding instead of having the cover art replicated on the boards. "I wanted a child to be able to remove the jacket and to have a book that then felt or appeared like a book for an older kid," Stead said, heralding the idea that although the picture book form may imply a shared reading transaction, individual child readers may stake claim to certain treasured picture books, wishing to make them their own well into their independent reading years. If you want to see a whale again and again, she asserted, just take off this book jacket and you won't need to feel self-conscious about reading a book that others might erroneously think is too young for you.

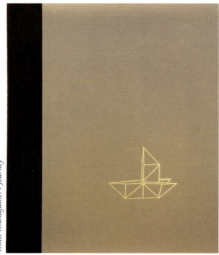

from Grandfather's Journey

Allen Say's *Grandfather's Journey* includes not a whale but the origami boat from the back of its jacket as a foil-stamped line drawing on the front board of the cover. When I've removed the jacket to show this to children at storytime, they've embraced the idea of the boat or ship as a recurring motif in the book and have then delighted in observing the times that boats appear in the book's illustrations. One day a class of first graders took their consideration of this embellishment on the front board of the cover a step further: as I held the front and back boards of the cover open, they noticed the emptiness of the back and the position of the origami boat on the front.

"Now you can see how far that boat went," a little girl exclaimed, recalling that in the jacket art the boat was on the back, but she now saw it on the front.

"Yeah, it's like the boat is sailing around the cover into the book," remarked a classmate.

The notion that jacket art (or in this case, foil-stamped cover art) invites the reader to open up the book and see what's inside is one that I try to capitalize on in Whole Book Approach storytimes. Rather than supporting the child's engagement with my own comments about what the story is about before I read the book, I try to use jacket and cover art to invite children to make their own observations and predictions and to pose their own questions.

Examining clothbound hardcover books by artists such as Allen Say is a great way to begin to explore how foil-stamped, blind-stamped, or ink-stamped art on the casing of a picture book informs overall design and enriches one's experience as a viewer. Take a gander at the boards of Chris Van Allsburg's picture books, and you'll find the bells from the Polar Express and the eponymous two bad ants on the boards of their respective picture books. Picture books by

> I try to use jacket and cover art to invite children to make their own observations and predictions and to pose their own questions.

David Wiesner, David Macaulay, and Barry Moser, among many other artists, also include such embellishments on the boards of hardcover editions. Simply pointing out these design elements and asking children what they see and how it connects to various observations and questions about jacket art can extend and enhance their visual experience of the form, as the ensuing conversations deepen children's engagement with picture books by literally *uncovering* their insights into picture book art and design.

Chapter 3

Visual Overtures

Endpapers

The picture book at the heart of my earliest story-times in schools and libraries on behalf of the Eric Carle Museum of Picture Book Art was not *Madeline*, or *Grandfather's Journey*, or *City Dog, Country Frog*, or any of the other titles I've mentioned thus far; instead, Bill Martin Jr. and Eric Carle's *Brown Bear, Brown Bear, What Do You See?* emerged as the perfect choice. While its illustrator was one obvious reason I chose the book—I was representing Eric Carle's museum, after all— I also liked the title's focus on talking about what one could see, and I appreciated the simplicity of the art and text and the attendant openness it afforded to storytime discussion about the visual aspects of the book.

I began with the endpapers. While the most immediate design elements to capture a reader's attention may be orientation, trim size, and jacket and cover art, I wanted to draw attention to endpapers as a design element that might otherwise get short shrift. If a picture book jacket is akin to the coming-attraction poster hanging outside the theater to invite the audience in, then the endpapers (the pages pasted onto the inside of the boards of a hardcover book) are the overture—not an auditory overture to a film's score, but a visual overture to the art of the book. What would children at storytime say if I simply pointed out the endpapers in *Brown Bear* and used open-ended questions to prompt their reflections on the bright, horizontal bars of color?

"These are the endpapers of the picture book," I would say. "They are glued onto the inside of the boards of the book cover, and often they give you clues about the artwork inside the book. What do you see happening on these endpapers for *Brown Bear*?"

When I first said something along these lines, I simply observed children looking at the endpapers and saying that they

from *Brown Bear, Brown Bear, What Do You See?*

saw lots of colors. I was satisfied and connected this observation to the book's function as a concept book: naming and showing colors to the reader. I didn't realize how very much I was missing until one day when I slowed down enough to let a child expand upon this observation, and I heard, "That's the order of the colors of the animals in the book."

The other children nodded, but I just sat there staring at the endpapers myself. Here was a book I'd read to my son and to many other children in museum and library programs hundreds (thousands?) of times, and yet I had never noticed this fact about the endpapers. I'd noticed that the endpapers comprised Carle's palette for the pictures, but I'd never recognized that they were a graphic table of contents.

> **I didn't realize how very much I was missing until one day when I slowed down enough to let a child expand upon this observation.**

"You're absolutely right!" I exclaimed, and I rededicated myself to listening—really listening—to what children had to say about the books I read with them instead of just listening for them to say things that I'd already considered.

This commitment came in handy during a later storytime that I led in a kindergarten classroom. Just as our discussion about the *Brown Bear* endpapers was winding down, a little girl piped up and said, "I see a sunset."

I'd never heard *that* before, so I asked, "What do you see that makes you say you see a sunset here?"

"At the top it's all dark and then the red and yellow are the setting sun, and then the blue is like water, and the green is grass, and then the purple is flowers, and then the white and black are maybe a road . . ." She sort of petered out at that point. But her representational reading of a landscape into Carle's abstract endpaper composition set the stage for an hour-and-fifteen-minute reading of *Brown Bear* as children went on to imagine the animals depicted in the book frolicking

> **I rededicated myself to listening—really listening—to what children had to say.**

about in the endpaper landscape, seeing each other. It didn't matter to them that, with the exception of the white dog, the pages with the animals have white backgrounds. They talked about the red bird flying in the sunset sky, the blue horse looking down on the green frog in the grass, and the goldfish swimming in the water.

While this classroom of children had reveled at the chance to creatively link Carle's abstract endpaper art to the content of the book proper, artists such as Steven Kellogg in his version of *Jack and the Beanstalk* sometimes use the front endpapers as space to establish a visual backstory to the narrative, or to begin the story before the opening words of the text. Another example of such an effective use of narrative content in picture book endpapers can be found in Candace Fleming and G. Brian Karas's sublime *Clever Jack Takes the Cak*e. The front endpapers show the palace messenger riding on horseback past Clever Jack's home, a loose invitation to the princess's birthday party falling from his sack. This paratextual illustration sets the story in motion, and then the closing endpapers show Jack and the princess walking along together after becoming friends at the party.

Other picture books use the endpapers to introduce an important motif or object in a story. In Kevin Henkes's *Wemberly Worried*, the front endpapers are decorated with many depictions of Wemberly's beloved doll, Petal. By book's end Wemberly has befriended a fellow preschooler who also has a cherished doll, named Nibblet. The back endpapers show the two dolls together, symbolizing the nascent friendship of their owners.

Akin to thematically driven color choices for a book's casing (as in the example in the previous chapter of Julie Fogliano and Erin Stead's *If You Want to See a Whale*), even endpapers that are a single color can provoke responses in children as they make meaning of this design choice and tie it to the content of the book as a whole. I often ask children to "make a color connection" between the jacket art and the color of the endpapers. They might see the connection in the color of the protagonist's clothing, or in some other important feature of the art. There is an aesthetic reason for this, of course—the endpapers in some way match the overall palette of the art in order to produce a cohesive look—but there is also logic to the design, since the endpapers cue the eye to look for a particular color in the interior artwork as they ease the viewer into the book proper.

For example, the yellow color of Marla Frazee's endpapers in her picture book version of the song "Hush, Little Baby" connects to the dress of the little girl on the front of the jacket. She emerges as the protagonist of the book, a jealous big sister who must try to hush her baby brother

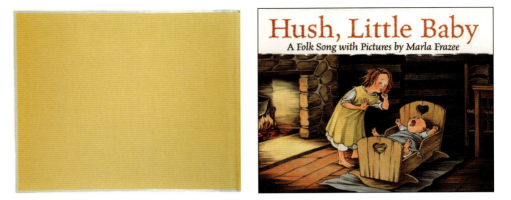

after she makes him cry. Frazee not only uses yellow to highlight the girl in her compositions; many of the things named in the song to hush the baby are also cast in yellow. The endpapers thus train the eye to look for these objects on the pages as the girl and her family spend a sleepless night trying to hush their crying baby.

As this example demonstrates, even the simplest of endpapers can play an integral role in illuminating the visual world of the picture book. And yet, further attention to front-matter paratexts reveals that the endpapers are only the beginning.

Chapter 4

Slow Down and Look

Front Matter

The genius of Marla Frazee's work in *Hush, Little Baby* does not end with its yellow endpapers. After all, the lullaby itself is not a story—it's a list of nonsensical items suggested to soothe a crying baby, reading a bit like the delirious musings of a sleep-deprived parent in the middle of the night. The story I outline above, about a jealous little girl who makes her baby brother cry and must hush him, is not actually part of the song's lyrics, nor is it part of Frazee's picture book text. Frazee crafts a story around the listing of a diamond ring, looking glass, billy goat, and so on, by infusing her artwork with narrative content that constructs characters, introduces drama, and brings the whole book to a satisfying, logical conclusion. She begins not in the book proper with the start of the song lyrics, but in the front matter.

The first illustration after the endpapers is a full-bleed picture depicting a little girl and her family walking away from the viewer. Since it's on the recto, it doesn't follow the traditional design of a frontispiece, which in book design terms is a verso picture facing a recto title page (see, for example, Trina Schart Hyman's brilliantly metafictive frontispiece for *Little Red Riding Hood*, in which the protagonist sits reading a book that looks just like the one the reader is holding). Instead, Frazee's wordless first illustration for *Hush Little Baby* occupies the typical placement of a half-title page—it precedes all other front-matter pages. In the image, the girl is turning to look back at a loaded-down horse and cart standing in front of a small building. A man resembling Santa Claus sits nearby on the front steps of the building near the cart. The page turn reveals a double-spread full title page with a different setting and a closer shot of the interior of a rustic cabin. The girl in the yellow dress stands on the far side of the verso page in an open doorway, casting a dark shadow across the room. Her arms are

from Little Red Riding Hood

crossed, and she scowls with her gaze fixed on the tender action of her parents tucking the baby into his cradle on the recto page.

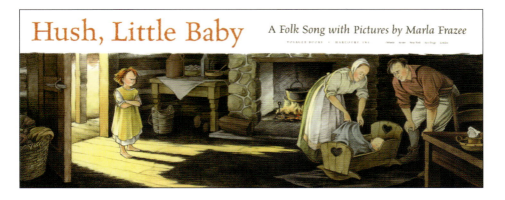

The page turn reveals the provocative culmination of the drama building in these wordless front-matter scenes: a vignette illustration on the dedication page, depicting the girl giving the cradle an angry shove, tells us why the baby needs hushing. The book proper then begins with the line, "Hush, little baby, don't say a word," which becomes not a parent's soothing verse

Hush, little baby, don't say a word,

sung to a tired baby, but a sister's pleading as she tries to cover her tracks and make things right again.

As the story progresses, the little girl brings her father to the man with the horse and cart, whom we viewed in the opening full-bleed illustration immediately following the endpapers. Lo and behold, he has all sorts of interesting things that might work to quiet the crying baby. In the end the parents resort to that familiar solution, going for a drive, to get their baby to sleep, but Frazee doesn't allow the bumpy ride in the horse and cart to quell his cries. Instead, keeping her focus on the child protagonist, when "that horse and cart fall down," Frazee depicts the sister catching her baby brother. Safe in her arms, he drifts off to sleep as the yellow sun rises in the background.

I once had an undergraduate student write a disastrous paper about this picture book because she had skipped over the crucial front-matter pages and gone directly to the book proper. Without the front matter's backstory about the sister's jealousy provoking her to shove the cradle, the student ended up writing about the baby as a "brat" who wouldn't stop crying no matter what his patient parents and sister did. The lesson from this misstep? Front matter matters.

Front matter matters.

As another example, consider the crucial role that front-matter pages play in Laura Vaccaro Seeger's *Bully*. Although, again, not a traditional verso frontispiece, a full-bleed spread immediately preceding the title-page spread shows a big, gray bull yelling "GO AWAY!" at the protagonist, a brown bull that is first depicted on the cover. This hurtful rejection sets the brown bull on his path of bullying others in the ensuing pages, importantly establishing "not an excuse, but . . . a reason" for his behavior, to quote Seeger.[20]

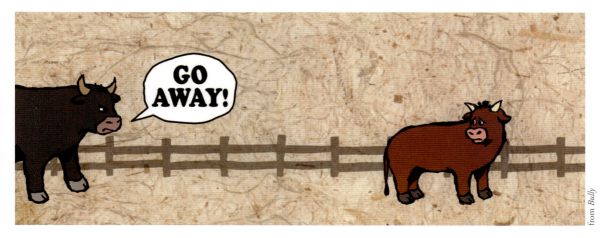

from *Bully*

Incorporating front-matter pages into Whole Book Approach storytimes simply requires taking the time to point out the different pages by name (this is the dedication page, this is the title page, and so on) and letting children respond to any art or design elements that catch their attention. This can sometimes lead to unexpected responses. Once I was reading Eric Carle's *The Very Hungry Caterpillar* at storytime, and we had a terrific discussion about the endpapers and how they reveal Carle's painted tissue-paper collage technique. The brightly colored collaged tissue papers have holes punched into them, revealing the white paper underneath or showing the papers as they overlap one another.

"Those are the holes that the caterpillar ate through," said one child, making a connection between the design of these abstract endpapers and the actual holes punched through the pages of the book.

from *The Very Hungry Caterpillar*

Another child took his peer's observation to its logical conclusion when we turned to the title page and saw the brightly colored paper dots lined across the bottom half of the page.

"So those dots are what he poops out after eating all those holes, right?" he asked.

Although I'm certain that's not what Eric Carle was thinking when he took the paper circles punched out of the endpaper tissue papers and glued them to the title page, the suggestion sure prompted a lot of giggles and plenty of eagerness to slow down and look so that we could engage more deeply with the art and design of this picture book.

So much can emerge from a consideration of paratexts. In their book *How Picturebooks Work*, Maria Nikolajeva and Carole Scott devote an entire chapter to picture book paratexts, noting:

> *Almost nothing has been written about the paratexts of picturebooks such as titles, covers, or endpapers. These elements are, however, still more important in picturebooks than in novels. If the cover of a children's novel serves as a decoration and at best can contribute to the general first impact, the cover of a picturebook is often an integral part of the narrative, especially when the cover picture does not repeat any of the pictures inside the book. The narrative can indeed start on the cover, and it can go beyond the last page onto the back cover. Endpapers can convey essential information, and pictures on title pages can both complement and contradict the narrative. . . . The contribution of paratexts to the picturebook is clearly highly significant, especially since they frequently carry a substantial percentage of the book's verbal and visual information. We find it interesting that this aspect has generally been neglected by critics.*[21]

It is indeed interesting that paratexts have generally been neglected by critics—especially since paratexts themselves are often so crucial to the cohesion of a story. Inviting children to mine those paratexts for meaning at the beginning of a storytime sets the stage for rich engagement with the illustrations, paired with text, in the book proper.

Chapter 5

Knocked Out by Type

Typography

S o where to turn, now that we've already done so much with the parts of the book outside of the book proper? Let's begin with the words—or actually, with the typography, or the arrangement and design of the words on the page. The written word is a visual representation of oral speech—this is a basic tenet of early literacy, and it's a wonder to behold a child taking steps toward recognizing this principle. A nanny I know told me of his experience reading Mo Willems's *What's Your Sound, Hound the Hound?* with his two-year-old charge, Jackson. He told me that when they reached the page where the cow says "moo," they saw that the text stretches out the sound across the spread. "I asked Jackson how he thought I should say the long word for the cow's sound, and instead of saying a long 'moo,' he pointed to each letter, saying it distinctly: five *m*'s and fourteen *o*'s."[22] Perhaps this isn't the reading Willems intended, but it was surely a worthwhile one in this toddler's burgeoning print awareness.

from What's Your Sound, Hound the Hound?

Often, the first letters a child recognizes are those in his or her name, particularly the first letter of the first name. When my daughter Caroline was a toddler, she proudly identified *c* as "her" letter, and she sought it out in the books we read together. Later, when she started learning more about letters representing sounds, she proudly said, "My letter, *c*, is so special because it shares two sounds with other letters: *sss* with *s* and *kuh* with *k*."

Clearly Caroline's phonemic awareness was growing, but written words obviously communicate more than the sounds of the letters or even the possible meanings of specific words. They also communicate tone, and typographic choices often play key roles in determining that element of written language. If a child who is learning to read must first understand that letters stand for sounds and that those sounds create words on a page, it follows that decisions around typography, or *how* the words are visually presented on the page—their typeface, their size, their placement on the page, and so on—will influence a reader's experience of the visual representation of speech. As scholars Frank Serafini and Jennifer Clausen note, "the typography of written language not only serves as a conduit of verbal narrative . . . it serves as a visual element and semiotic resource with its own meaning potentials."[23]

Although David Wiesner may be regarded as the veritable king of wordless picture books, his Caldecott Medal winner *The Three Pigs* has a text that demanded careful typesetting. His acceptance speech for the medal recounts the crucial role of type in picture book design:

> *When I've made books with few or no words, it seemed I left my art director, Carol Goldenberg, with seemingly little to do. This, of course, was not true. But it did often leave very little typesetting, something I know she loves. With* The Three Pigs *I decided to make up for all those years of neglect and see how many ways I could distort, crumple, and scatter the text to create a typesetting nightmare for her. In the end, it was fun. Painful, but fun. For her years of insight, commiseration, and*

always welcome input, I dedicated The Three Pigs *to Carol.*[24]

Although Wiesner is referring to the text in the book proper, jackets can also provide great jumping-off points for inviting children to consider the impact of typography, since as previously discussed, they act like posters to grab the reader's attention. Scholar Barbara Z. Kiefer relates the following fascinating story of a child's observations about the particular typeface used on two book jackets:

> *One first grader argued that* Mother, Mother, I Want Another *by Maria Polushkin was illustrated by the same artist who did* I Saw a Ship A-Sailing *[Domanska]. I was puzzled by his conviction because the two books differed greatly in artistic style. Perhaps the fact that there was a mouse on each book helped make the connection? "No" he explained, "The words." I still did not understand because the words in the titles were different. As I looked more closely, however, I discovered that both books had been set in Abbott Old Style, a rather distinctive typeface. The student had, in fact, over-generalized the style of the printed letters to the entire art work.*[25]

One time my daughter Caroline indulged not in that kind of over-generalization but in what might be regarded as over-specification after reading my good friend David Hyde Costello's picture book *Little Pig Joins the Band*. In addition to its main narrative text, the spreads include

hand-lettered intraiconic text with tails to indicate dialogue. Seeing this, Caroline was inspired to incorporate
this technique into her own artwork. "It's just like how
David did his book, Mom-Mom," she told me. And then

from *Little Pig Joins the Band*

for quite some time after that, whenever she saw a picture
book using this technique (or speech balloons of the sort
David would go on to use in the picture book I authored, *A
Crow of His Own*) she would say, "They must've gotten that
idea from David's Little Pig book."

from *A Crow of His Own*

One of the first picture books I used in Whole Book Approach storytimes to engage children with typography was Anthony Browne's *Voices in the Park*, which doesn't use speech balloons to indicate its characters' voices, but instead employs diverse typeface choices. This picture book homage to surrealist art, with particular references to René Magritte's works, tells the story of a day in the park from four different characters' perspectives. The typography on the jacket immediately introduces readers to a central design concept of the book: its use of four different typefaces to differentiate the four characters' voices. Here, the word "Voices" uses those typefaces, and then the rest of the title—"in the Park"—appears in a single typeface to represent the setting that unites the characters.

Meanwhile, on the back of the jacket, a single line of text from each character is printed in its respective typeface. Once when I asked a group of children to describe how the way the words looked might tell me how to read each voice aloud, one child zeroed in on the line of text from the shy little boy character (well, he's actually an anthropomorphic chimp, since this is a Browne title) and said that his words looked like "a whisper on the page." Indeed, the section of the book told through his character is printed in faint type that evokes his quiet, shy nature as he struggles to resist the domineering force of his mother. Her voice, on the other hand, is printed in a traditional typeface that one might expect to find in a primer and that expresses her disapproval of the "very rough-looking child" whom her son befriends.

Laura Vaccaro Seeger has reflected on how children respond to typography in discussing her own picture book about friendship overcoming bullying behavior (*Bully*, noted in the previous chapter). The spare text is presented as speech-balloon dialogue between the protagonist bull and other animals. The bully's words grow larger as the bull ramps up his cruelty, until a determined goat gives him what-for. At a dinner hosted by her publisher at the American Library Association's annual conference in 2013, Seeger recounted how she invites children to read the text aloud. "The great thing is that kids know that the bigger the word is, the louder their voices should be, and vice versa," she said. But the insights into typography and its impact on verbal expression don't stop there. When the heroic goat shames the bully of a bull and the bull apologizes, Seeger said that she asks the children if they believe that the bull is really sorry. And they do. They read sincerity into his apology because of the small tear

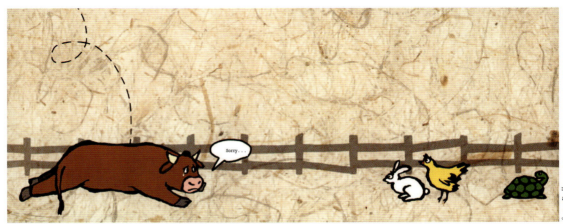

from *Bully*

rolling from his eye, yes, but also because the single word of text, "Sorry . . . ," appears small on the page, especially compared to the larger words bursting with bullish bravado that precede it in the text.

Sometimes reading text in a voice that *opposes* the sort of tone a particular typographic choice might suggest can be a great way to get children talking about the expressive nature of type. This happened once when I read *A Visitor for Bear* by Bonny Becker, with illustrations by Kady MacDonald Denton, at a storytime at a public library, and my dramatic side got the best of me. I really got into expressing curmudgeonly Bear's dismay at the persistent visitations of the "small and gray and bright-eyed" mouse, loudly yelling out "BEGONE!" A child attending the storytime looked at me and said sternly and quietly, "You know, you really shouldn't yell in the library."

Upon hearing this admonition, I, of course, thought of Michelle Knudsen and Kevin Hawkes's superb *Library Lion*, which grapples with this very rule in its story, but instead of making that intertextual connection, I decided

from *A Visitor for Bear*

to fall back on the typographic choices in Becker and Denton's book.

"You're right," I told the boy who'd challenged my reading. "You usually shouldn't yell in a library." I shrugged. "But the book made me do it." And then I turned to the larger group and asked, "Why did I just *have* to yell that word?"

Another child raised her hand and said, "Because that word is so big, and it's in all capital letters."

And indeed, it is.

"Think of how silly it would be if I read that word aloud in a very quiet, gentle voice," I told the group. And then I did so, barely whispering, perhaps with a slight British affectation—"*Begone . . .*"—and the children laughed uproariously.

I've used similar tactics when reading Jon Scieszka and Lane Smith's *The Stinky Cheese Man and Other Fairly Stupid Tales*, adopting a soft, lilting tone when reading the Little Red Hen's dialogue aloud. The type assigned to her voice is bold, red, and sans serif and demands to be read in a loud, harsh voice. Deliberately resisting such a voice and then asking kids to correct the tone I use gets them thinking about the impact of typographic choices on tone and meaning.

In stark contrast with the striking and varied typography decisions in *The Stinky Cheese Man*, Leonard S. Marcus notes in a *Horn Book Magazine* article cleverly entitled "Give 'Em Helvetica," that "harmoniousness and understatement are clearly among the watchwords in picture-book type selection and design."[26] In other words, another design approach to picture books that departs from that used in *The Stinky Cheese Man* and *A Visitor for Bear* suggests that rather than being an overt and obvious part of the visual element of the book, the printed word shouldn't be a distraction from the art; it should seamlessly integrate into the visual layout of the page. How to achieve this? A

Deliberately resisting such a voice and then asking kids to correct the tone I use gets them thinking about the impact of typographic choices.

lot depends on whether the art on the page is framed (more on that in a moment), but in the case of full-bleed art that extends out to all sides of a page, the type must be especially well integrated into the design of the page. Jerry Pinkney's nearly wordless Caldecott Medal winner, *The Lion & the Mouse*, incorporates various intraiconic, ono-matopoeic sounds (owl hoots, the sounds of a jeep driving through the African savannah, and, of course, squeaking mice and a lion's roar). This creates a text that functions something like a soundtrack, which allows readers to im-merse themselves in the setting he's created.

Another favorite example of such seamless integration of text arises not from the use of intraiconic text, but from artful accommodation of narrative text, in Trina Schart Hyman's version of *The Sleeping Beauty*. This old fairy tale about a girl crossing the threshold to womanhood has archways, windows, doors, mirrors, and patches of sky that seamlessly provide open spaces in the illustrations for blocks of text. In his very different fairy-tale retelling of *Goldilocks and the Three Bears*, James Marshall similarly

from *The Sleeping Beauty*

uses a mirror to hold the text in one of the crowded interior scenes set in the Three Bears' house.

I don't recall a child ever commenting on this sort of design choice, perhaps because in storytimes children are less likely to look at words than they are at pictures; they

from *Goldilocks and the Three Bears*

listen to the text read aloud and combine the oral reading with the art they see to form what Jane Doonan calls "the composite text"[27] in their minds. Or perhaps this is just an area that I haven't devoted as much attention to in my own practice so far. This is certainly an emerging area of picture book criticism, and in their essay "Typography as Semiotic Resource," Frank Serafini and Jennifer Clausen analyze the following typographic features in five selected picture books: weight, color, size, slant, framing, formality, and flourishes.[28] While my own work doesn't go into as much detail as theirs does with regard to particular picture books, the anecdotal documentation of children's responses to typography that I've gathered marks this area of inquiry as one with rich potential for further exploration.

As I contemplate this potential, I can also recall many instances where children with new reading skills were eager to read words aloud—particularly when they appear in large type on the page. Time and again while reading *Yo! Yes?* by Chris Raschka, for example, I've felt as if I was in an echo chamber—I'd say "Yo!" and the group would say "Yo!"; I'd say "Yes?" and they'd say "Yes?" Rather than discouraging this echoing, I often would fade away from reading the simple text myself and point to the words on the page, inviting the children to perform a choral reading of the text. This in turn provoked discussion about how punctuation, design choices regarding type size and color, and the words' interactions with the pictures combined to communicate this story about new friendship.

Even pre-readers who cannot yet decode words on the

page have delivered strong insights into typographic design choices. Once while I was reading *Brown Bear, Brown Bear, What Do You See?* with a preschool class, a three-year-old commented that the spread with the white dog, which has a black background (unlike all the other spreads, which have white backgrounds), needs white lettering "or else the words would be camouflaged if they were still black." Here, a child who could not yet read words for meaning was commenting on an essential principle of visual art—that, in the words of Molly Bang, "contrast enables us to see."[29] The design term for using white type on a dark background is "knockout type," and this child's teachers and I were, indeed, knocked out by her intuitive understanding of this concept.

While we might be inclined to think of children opening their ears to words read aloud at storytime, opening their eyes to see the expressive nature of the visible text on the page affords new opportunities for engagement in Whole Book Approach storytimes. Typography, however, is only one of a myriad of choices in page design that can and do provide readers with opportunities to make meaning of all they see.

Chapter 6

Gutter Talk and More

Page Design

Picture book scholar Barbara Bader's assertion that the success of the picture book "as an art form . . . hinges on the interdependence of pictures and words, on the simultaneous display of two facing pages, and on the drama of the turning of the page"[30] provokes consideration of the interaction between words and pictures, the impact of page-layout decisions on a reading, and the great importance of pacing in the picture book form. Although there are many possible avenues to pursue, the main page-design elements I've asked children to consider in Whole Book Approach storytimes concern how artists accommodate or even employ the book gutter, the use or absence of frames, and the dynamic between verso and recto pages.

First, a little gutter talk. Though rarely acknowledged in critical discussions of picture book art, the gutter—the vertical seam between the verso and recto pages, where the pages of the picture book are bound together—plays a tremendously important role in informing the display of facing pages and helps the reader progress toward, or resist the pull of, the page turn. This production element necessarily impacts the success of the design of each page opening because it dips down into the binding, creating an interruption of the picture space. Attending not only to how artists accommodate the gutter in their compositions but also to how they use the gutter to enhance a visual separation between the verso and recto pages emerges as a fascinating part of Whole Book Approach storytimes.

The first thing to acknowledge about facing pages is that artists can decide whether to illustrate single- or double-page spreads; in other words, they can decide whether their art will cross the gutter or not at a particular page opening. This decision impacts the pacing of the page turns and of the visual narrative. Think of it this way: part of Bader's "drama of the turning of the page" rests upon understanding the page turn in a picture book as the passage of time, and upon regarding the picture book as a sequential work of art in which one picture leads to the next. Not all picture books follow explicitly linear plots in which every page progresses chronologically from event to event in the

> **[The gutter] helps the reader progress toward, or resist the pull of, the page turn.**

narrative, but most do. The artist must decide whether to compress time or to expand it before the reader moves toward the turn of the page.

Typically, an image that crosses the gutter into double-spread art expands time and invites the reader to linger on the larger picture. If space equals time, it's as though the picture is taking a long time (taking up a lot of space) to say what it needs to say. This effect is enhanced when a wordless double-page picture occurs at the climax of a story, evoking a contemplative moment for the reader to reflect upon the scene and relate it back to the words and images that preceded it. Brian Selznick frequently includes this sort of page design in books he illustrates. See, for example, the wordless spread at the heart of *When Marian Sang* by Pam Muñoz Ryan, which depicts Marian Anderson's Easter Sunday concert on the steps of the Lincoln Memorial.

from *When Marian Sang*

A double-page spread needn't be wordless, however, to create the same time-stretching effect and to provoke the reader to pause and take it all in. Patrick Benson's illustrations in *Mole and the Baby Bird* by Marjorie Newman are at first relegated to a single page, but starting with the page reading "Grandad took Mole to the top of a high hill," full-bleed, double-page art brings the reader into Mole's perspective as he thrills at the wide open sky before him and poignantly begins to reconsider his keeping of a wild bird as a pet in his "dark underground room."

When artists do choose to allow picture book art to cross the gutter, they must accommodate the loss of picture space that the gutter physically imposes on the picture plane. This fact posed a particular challenge in another of Brian Selznick's books, *The Invention of Hugo Cabret*, which won the 2008 Caldecott Medal. Selznick describes his book, more than five hundred pages long, as "not exactly a novel, not quite a picture book, not really a graphic novel, or a flip book or a movie, but a combination of all these things."[31] The sheer number of pages, many without text and devoted solely to illustration, meant that the book required a special production element to ensure that it would lie flat when opened, in order to prevent artwork from getting lost in the gutter. A loose-back Smyth-sewn binding (the sort often used in cookbooks) elegantly solved this problem.

Such a binding is rare in most storytime fare, with picture books most often using other production methods.

In Whole Book Approach storytimes, I often draw attention to the picture book gutter by holding it open and flat at the children's eye level so they can see how it dips down. I then ask them to think about where else they've heard the word *gutter*, and someone usually mentions bowling.

"How do you feel if your ball goes into the gutter?" I ask.

"Bad!" is the standard response (though many children helpfully suggest the use of bumpers to prevent gutter balls).

"Yes," I continue, "and just like bowlers don't want the bowling ball to go into the gutter, artists don't want im-portant parts of their pictures to fall into the book gutter, either. So let's look at how they keep this from happening."

One image I often return to for this discussion is Eric Carle's picture of the teacher in *Brown Bear, Brown Bear, What Do You See?* Note that all the preceding pictures of animals are horizontally oriented and thus fit with their midsections falling on the line of the gutter. The human teacher is the first vertically oriented figure in the book and thus posed a compositional challenge for Carle. In order to maintain the double-page layout, he does not show the teacher's entire body, instead bringing her into close perspective and allowing her figure to break the page.

Once, I had planned to use Whole Book Approach questions to prompt a discussion about how Carle accommodates the gutter of the book in this picture of the teacher, but instead the group ended up talking about something else—how art can bleed off a page. This picture always gets a big reaction—"She looks mean!" is a frequent response, or "Why is she so angry?" or "Her lipstick is funny!" I'd heard all of these comments and slight variations many times. But on this particular day, a little boy looked at the picture of the teacher and announced, "She has a really flat hairdo."

I immediately understood his misperception and bit my tongue to keep from laughing out loud as I wondered how many other children have struggled with this page's composition and have come to similar conclusions about the teacher's bad hair day. *I* look at this picture and imagine that she has a bun in the back that forces the hair at the front of her head to pouf up. But this child looking at it thought that the teacher had a flattop because we cannot see the top of the pouf; we must imagine it rising up beyond the confines of the page.

gutter

Teacher,
Teacher,
What do you see?

I see children
looking at me.

from *Brown Bear, Brown Bear, What Do You See?*

"Hmmm . . . ," I said. "Look at the bottom of the picture. Does her body end right there, or does she have more body outside of the picture?"

"No one just has shoulders. You'd be dead," another child said, giving me a withering look.

"Right," I continued. "So, does she have to have such a flat hairdo, or can you imagine a style that goes up beyond the edge of the top of the page?"

"She has an Afro!" another child said.

"No. She has Texas hair," said yet another preschooler, and with these humorous descriptions I realized that the children could visualize how the image of the teacher extended beyond her depicted form.

This sort of visualization can also be provoked by art that is confined by a frame. For example, in *John Henry*, written by Julius Lester and illustrated by Jerry Pinkney, early illustrations show the entire figure of John Henry as an infant and child within the confines of the framed pictures, but once he achieves his full-grown, immense stature, the art never depicts his entire form again. Instead, the body of this legendary, larger-than-life protagonist breaks the frame, and the viewer must understand that the rest of his body exists outside of the picture plane. This method emphasizes his tall stature and also expresses the grandeur of his spirit in a story that leaves readers with this message: "Dying ain't important. Everybody does that. What matters is how well you do your living."

Meanwhile, Martin and Carle's *Brown Bear* isn't preoccupied with delivering such a message or even telling a story—it's most often used as a concept book about colors. But, reading this deceptively simple picture book with children has shown me time and again that what matters is how well we do our looking.

Let's turn back to the picture of the teacher, which deviates from others in layout because Carle does not center the image on the double-spread—he can't, because he must accommodate the gutter. Centrally placing the teacher's face in the double-spread would bisect it. By shifting the teacher's face to the recto page, he allows the gutter to fall along the natural line of her jaw instead of awkwardly down the middle of her face.

When I've asked children to look at this picture and describe how they see Carle making room for the gutter, they've often used their own bodies to physically show or act out a sideways movement with their own heads and necks, as though they were avoiding having their own faces bisected by a book gutter. (As an aside, attending to children's nonverbal, physical expressions is often a key part of Whole Book Approach storytimes, since I so often see children struggling to find the right words and instead using their bodies to respond to pictures. My favorite example is a toddler who shrugged his shoulders up and down in imitation of the movement of the Very Hungry Caterpillar on the cover of Eric Carle's famed picture book.) One child even used her hand to squish her cheeks together, saying, "If the teacher was in the gutter, she'd look like this."

If we turn again to the title page of Marla Frazee's *Hush,*

Little Baby, we can see an example of a picture that not only accommodates but makes use of the gutter in its composition.

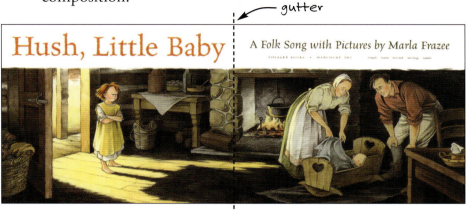

"Those parents are like a circle of love around the baby, and the sister is all the way over there on the other page," remarked a preschooler when I read this book with her class (and oh, I just knew that she was the oldest child in *her* family). Indeed, by placing the jealous girl on the verso and the other characters on the recto, with the gutter between them, Frazee heightens the dramatic tension of the picture to a degree that merely separating them in a single-page illustration would not achieve.

This is just one instance where the gutter is not merely the physical site of the binding, or a facet of book production that must be accommodated in order to avoid having it interrupt the visual continuity of a double-page spread. It's another physical and visual component of the book for readers to consider as they engage with the picture book as an art form. Similarly, Chris Raschka isolates his two

gutter

gutter

from *Yo! Yes?*

characters in *Yo! Yes?* on facing pages with the gutter between them. This holds true until the story's resolution, when the shy child on the recto page accepts the other boy's gesture of friendship and joins him on the verso. In a feat of perfect pacing that started with a single recto title page, the book ends with a single verso-page illustration depicting the boys jumping hand-in-hand in an exuberant celebration of their new friendship.

Raschka underscores the boys' bond on the final page by also merging the white spaces that had acted as separate spotlights amid expressive washes of color on previous pages. The culminating page design visually asserts a heartwarming resolution to the story, but it still keeps the viewer at a distance, since even the now-merged white space around the characters acts as a visual reminder of the separation between the world of the book and the world of the reader.

from *Yo! Yes?*

Ultimately, using a frame or border to enclose an image, or surrounding it by negative space (as in *Yo! Yes?*), impacts the viewer's perception. For example, like the animals depicted before her in the book, the teacher in Carle's *Brown Bear, Brown Bear, What Do You See?* is not enclosed by a frame. Carle simply situates the figures in this book against empty white space (or, in the case of the white dog, empty black space), creating a presentation of the art that is free of visual barriers between the viewer and the pictures. The impact welcomes viewers into the world of the book, making them participants rather than spectators.

This effect is even more pronounced when fully detailed backgrounds bleed off the page without a frame enclosing them within the picture plane. A full-bleed page design results in a dynamic, inviting presentation that obscures awareness of the perceptual line between the reader's reality and the world of the book, creating a greater sense of intimacy in the reading. For example, Aaron Becker uses this technique to great advantage in his Caldecott Honor Book *Journey*, immersing the

from *Journey*

reader in full-bleed fantastic landscapes at key points in his protagonist's adventure as she moves from one setting to another and brings the reader along with her. When he visited a course I was teaching, Becker said that his framing choices were inspired by his study of *Where the Wild Things Are*, in which Maurice Sendak famously uses diminishing and expanding air frames (white space around the picture, without any lines or decorative embellishments to define the frame). This influence is quite apparent in the enclosed, small picture of the forlorn protagonist in her bedroom before she embarks on her adventures. Such framing decisions greatly inform the reader's perception of the art.

from Journey

When I read Sendak's book with children, I instruct them to "watch the air frames" and tell me what they notice. "The pictures are getting bigger" or "Max is getting bigger" or "all the white space is going away" are the sorts of responses I've heard again and again by the time we reach the third double-page spread and see an angry Max sent to his room. The conversations that ensue have related this effect to "zooming in like a movie," a comment that underscores the cinematic nature of Sendak's art. Other children have read meaning into the design, noting that Max looks trapped in the first picture, but that he seems more powerful as the pictures get bigger.

Of course, as the page turns progress, the pictures continue to get bigger, and eventually the art encroaches upon the air frame when the trees in Max's room branch out into the white space. When the wild rumpus starts, Sendak launches the reader into a series of three wordless, full-bleed spreads, the visual climax of the narrative. But there's more: white space returns at the bottom of the spread following the wild rumpus, when Max wants "to be where someone loved him best of all." It continues to expand, eventually relegating the art to the recto page, with Max returned to his bedroom, and preserving the verso for text. Here, the art is not enclosed by a frame—Max has tamed his wild things and no longer feels trapped.

> **The simple device of framing can enable the separation between the world of the reader and the world of the book to be either blurred or underscored.**

So much artistic expression is devoted to making the intangible feelings and ideas that make up our emotional lives visible or concrete. Time and again I've witnessed children engage with books in ways that take my breath away as they commune with characters—and by extension, the artists who created them—and learn about themselves as they bear witness, or seemingly participate in, wild rumpuses and the like. The simple device of framing can enable the separation between the world of the reader and the world of the book to be either blurred or underscored, manipulating the reader's response in deft and sure ways.

Perhaps the most affecting moment I've seen in this vein occurred not in my professional life but while reading at home with my children. My son Stevie had just turned six when the 2011 Caldecott committee (of which I was a member) awarded Laban Carrick Hill and Bryan Collier's *Dave the Potter: Artist, Poet, Slave* an honor. When we read the picture book together, we ended up talking quite a bit about the cruelty and injustices of slavery, and Stevie asked, "Why didn't they run away?"

"Some people did," I told him, and then we talked about Harriet Tubman and the Underground Railroad as I made a mental note to share some of the many books we own about that part of American history with Stevie and his siblings. His older sister Emilia was already familiar with Tubman's name and said that she was very brave for helping so many people escape to freedom.

"So did she get everybody except for Dave?" Stevie asked, his face falling as he thought about this particular person, one of myriad nameless people in his new, limited knowledge of this part of our history.

"No, she didn't get everybody; there were too many people to help. But she helped lots and lots of people," I explained.

Stevie shifted into a contemplative mood at that point, and at the end of our reading he asked to bring the book back to his bedroom. The next day I found him sitting on his bed with the book opened to its glorious, full-bleed, gatefold (or foldout) page depicting a sequence of Dave's hands throwing a pot. Stevie was poised over the pictures, fitting his own hands on top of Dave's, seemingly seeking to immerse himself even more deeply in the story. The image in my mind's eye was arresting enough, but risking

intrusion, I snapped a few photos, as well. Would Stevie have done this if the pictures were framed? Perhaps. But I can't help but think that the openness of the unframed, full-bleed art acted as an invitation of sorts for my son to commune more deeply with Dave the Potter. If this can happen during an independent reading

Megan Dowd Lambert's son Stevie

transaction of the sort I stumbled upon in my son's room, then it can surely happen in storytime, too. Whole Book Approach techniques of slowing a reading down to welcome responses to art, or of pointing out design elements like frames and gutters, and of just listening to what children say when we give them the chance to speak up during a reading can help ensure this.

Chapter 7

"Children, Children, What Do You See?"

Nurturing Visual Intelligence

As the preceding chapters on the parts of the picture book demonstrate, inviting children to share what they think and observe about paratexts and page layout provokes a deeper awareness of art and design during storytime. This, in turn, prompts consideration of how the visual and material elements of the picture book interact with and inform the reading of the verbal text. As was the case with my failure to see the endpapers in *Brown Bear, Brown Bear, What Do You See?* as a graphic table of contents, my experiences reading with children often left me positively gobsmacked as I confronted my own lack of awareness, poor visual engagement, and knee-jerk privileging of verbal text. Perhaps my most humbling Whole Book Approach storytime occurred when I was reading Leo Lionni's *Frederick* with a group of second graders, and our conversation enabled me to inch toward a new appreciation for this book about a little mouse with the heart of a poet.

We began the reading by spending a good deal of time discussing the jacket art and the endpapers, which have Frederick's name scrawled over and over upon them.

"Leo Lionni really wants us to know this book is about Frederick!" one child said, and I silently congratulated myself on having already appreciated how the lettering on the endpapers is printed to look like a signature (just like the title on the jacket and the repetition of the title on front-matter pages). This clever typographic choice underscores Frederick's individuality and the ultimate triumph of his unique poetic contribution to his family of field mice, and I felt premature pride at having gleaned such meaning myself as the children reinforced this reading.

As the storytime progressed, our careful attention to *Frederick*'s paratexts set the stage for the children to reflect on the interior illustrations and their interdependence with the text. On the fifth double-page spread, in response to the field mice's needling about his apparent sloth, Frederick announces that while they are busily gathering nuts to store for the winter, he is "gather[ing] colors . . . for winter is gray." The bottom of the page is sprinkled with small, colorful flowers, but the picture is dominated by the wintery gray that Frederick anticipates: large gray stones stretch across the facing pages, and Frederick sits on the wall they form with his back to the reader, while the field mice form a chain across the rest of the wall, hoisting nuts to one another. I asked the storytime group to talk about how the words and pictures work together to tell the story, and I anticipated that they, like me, and like other groups before them, would mention how the composition's focus on the gray stone wall and the gray mice anticipates the grayness of winter and therefore echoes Frederick's words.

And then a little boy said, "Well, Frederick is looking at the flowers to gather all those colors."

Hmm. I quickly assessed how to proceed. Frederick's back is quite clearly facing the flowers on the bottom of the page, so I thought that the child must have misunderstood the picture somehow. Maybe, sitting at a distance, he thought the rounded ears on top of Frederick's head were his eyes? Or maybe he had somehow identified a different mouse as Frederick?

"Do you mean that *this* mouse Frederick is looking at these flowers?" I asked, pointing to each on the page.

The boy gazed at me with patient pity.

"No," he replied. "Frederick has his back to us, and to those flowers, but he is gazing out at the meadow beyond the wall, and that's where all the flowers he sees are, I bet. We can't see them, and the other mice can't see them, but Frederick can."

I exhaled. Of course. The first line of text on this page reads, "And when they saw Frederick sitting there, staring at the meadow . . ."

I'd never realized what this little boy had so deftly pointed out. All at once I recognized myself as a blasted field mouse, diligently working away, pointing at pictures, reading text, asking questions, but never really seeing the art before me. Meanwhile, this child sitting in my story-time group was Frederick incarnate, allowing me and his classmates to see flowers and colors beyond the stone walls of our imaginative landscapes.

Moments such as this one with *Frederick* made me realize that there was a lot I wasn't seeing, and that my Whole Book Approach impulse to give children the time and space to share and explore all that they could see was sound. Not only did the method enrich their own group reading experiences, but it allowed me to see and appreciate picture books in ways I couldn't have achieved on my own, while also coming to recognize the sophisticated thinking that children bring to their encounters with visual images. For example, soon after the Eric Carle Museum of Picture Book Art opened and my graduate independent study turned into a full-fledged position in the museum's education department, a child at storytime piped up and said, "I know it's a flamingo, but it looks like an elephant."

I was reading Eric Carle's *10 Little Rubber Ducks* when the child voiced this observation, and although I'd come to pride myself on leading interactive storytimes and thinking on my feet when questions and comments seemed to come from left field, I was stumped by this child's statement. Holding the book out to face the group in front of me, I wondered if two creatures could be more *dissimilar* in appearance than a flamingo and an elephant. Hoping for

> **Moments such as this one with *Frederick* made me realize that there was a lot I wasn't seeing.**

some clarification, I resorted to my standard, open-ended response, gleaned from Visual Thinking Strategies.

"What do you see that makes you say that?"

"Well, the neck is all curved like an elephant's trunk, and the body is like the elephant's head looking sideways," observed the child.

"Yes," another child continued, "and the bent-up leg could sort of be like a tusk."

I looked at the picture and suddenly could see the elephantine profile for myself. We spent the rest of storytime talking about the other pictures in the book, breaking them down into their component shapes to see what might be hidden within Carle's brightly colored collages. I read the words of the story, too, but the child who'd seen the flamingo's inner elephant opened up a new way to consider the book's pictures even as they worked alongside the words of the story, and I marveled at the sophisticated thinking inherent in looking at representative art and rendering it into abstraction.

The **4**th little rubber duck drifts south. A flamingo stares at it.

from 10 Little Rubber Ducks

This example was an inverse of the experience the kindergarten group had with the *Brown Bear, Brown Bear, What Do You See?* endpapers, in which they read representational meaning (a sunset) into an abstract work of art (the horizontal bars of color). I can't take credit for the particular insights that these children realized, since they were born of their

70

own thinking. But bearing witness to them underscored my commitment to giving picture book art and design terminology to children and welcoming them to respond to all the parts of the picture book—the whole book— during our readings together. Furthermore, I came to regard the process as important not only to give children the time and space to point out unseen, flowery fields observed by a poet mouse, or to discover elephants lurking within flamingos, but also to support children in building the visual literacy skills they need to understand and create meaning from the art on the page when illustration conventions baffle them. After all, just as children must develop print awareness and other skills to be able to decode text and achieve fluency in their

> **Just as children need to develop print awareness and other skills to be able to decode text and achieve fluency in their reading of words, learning to read pictures is a skill that develops over time and exposure.**

reading of words, learning to read pictures is a skill that develops over time and exposure. In an article for the magazine *Book Links*, illustrator Chris Raschka writes:

> *Beyond appealing art, there is the art that advances, in the words of Rudolf Arnheim, "the child's intelligence of seeing." We're comfortable with the idea of a child's verbal intelligence growing with and by means of literature. But we tend to take visual intelligence for granted. Or we dismiss it as simply the routine camera-like function of the eye. But eyes are much more than*

this. They think. They learn. We know there is value in the intelligence of the eye, we have big museums dedicated to it, but we're not sure how to teach it. How do you teach color, form, line? You do it the same way you do words and sentences and ideas, by slowly increasing the level of complexity, depth and multi-layeredness. When the same care is taken in the use of formal elements of art—color and composition, for instance—as is demanded in art for adults, a child will inevitably become more visually intelligent, just as is the case in reading when care is taken in shaping the text of a story.[32]

Not only are Raschka's words a clarion call to illustrators, art directors, and publishers to provide children with great art, they are also an acknowledgment of the role that picture books can play in supporting a child's developing visual literacy skills. Providing the time and space during storytimes for children to voice the questions they have about how pictures work is not only potentially enriching, but also supportive of their overall comprehension and engagement in shared reading. After all, if children struggle to understand how words and pictures work together because of a misperception or a difficulty in following the visual narrative, how will they successfully stay engaged?

Reader-response theorists call misreadings of text "aberrant readings" and investigate how such readings arise by considering such variables as a text's flawed execution, a reader's limited schema, and tension or distance between the author's intended audience and the text's implied audience. The work of these critics starts with readers' (sometimes aberrant) responses and then moves back to interpret and critique the text, suggesting that meaning doesn't exist in the book or in the reader, but in the space between them. I try to bring this critical stance to Whole Book Approach storytimes and am careful not to assert myself as the authority with the right answer to correct aberrant readings; when a child misreads a picture or is clearly puzzled by it in some way, I steer the quandary back to the group. In his seminal developmental psychology text, *Mind in Society: The Development of Higher Psychological Processes*, L. S. Vygotsky postulated the theory of zones of proximal development. He suggested that we learn best from "collaboration with more capable peers."[33] This makes intuitive sense to me in that it seems less intimidating to learn something from someone who is closer to your own level of achievement or expertise than it is to learn from someone leaps and bounds ahead of you. My hope is that children at storytime will learn from one another if I facilitate the conversation and enable their collaborative reading of a picture book by using Visual Thinking Strategies questions ("What's going on in this picture? What do you see that makes you say that? What more can we find?") and then branching out into other open-ended questions such as:

"Can anyone else tell me more about this picture?"

"Does anyone have a different idea about this picture?"

Giving children the space to address aberrant readings as a group gives them the chance to, in the words of Ms. Frizzle from the Magic School Bus television series, "Take chances, make mistakes, get messy!" at storytime. In this way the storytime leader follows in Ms. Frizzle's footsteps as the epitome of a teacher who acts not as a "sage on the stage," to use the words of professor Alison King of California State University, but as a "guide on the side," with the picture book at the center.[34]

I sought to occupy such a role at a storytime at the Carle when I read Wanda Gág's classic picture book *Millions of Cats*. After the "hundreds of cats, thousands of cats, millions and billions and trillions of cats" devour each other in a fit of vanity (which occurs offstage, mercifully sparing the reader any visuals of this fantastic, cannibalistic feline massacre), only one skinny little kitten remains. The story's very old man and very old woman take the kitten in, and a double-page spread depicts a curved sequence of pictures of the kitten lapping up a bowl of milk. *I* look at the sequence and understand that it represents a compression of time on the picture plane—each image of the kitten marks a different day when she is drinking milk, getting a bit plumper and rounder as the images progress from left to right across the verso and recto pages. This design, called simultaneous succession or continuous narrative, is confusing for many children, who instead assume that multiple depictions of the same figure on a single page or spread means not that they are seeing one character over the passage of time but a whole group of characters together in one moment.

"So many cats, again?" asked a child looking at Gág's kitten lapping milk, clearly worried that the offstage, cannibalistic feline massacre was about to start up all over again. I immediately grasped this misunderstanding and tried to redirect the group back to a discussion about this picture before moving on to the next part of the text.

"There *are* a lot of kittens on this page, aren't there?" I responded. "Let's count them," and as I pointed to each image in the sequence, we did just that.

"But it's just the same cat getting fatter," said another child, and this peer response enabled the first child to breathe a sigh of relief and to understand what Gág meant to depict with her sequence of pictures showing the kitten at its bowl.

from Millions of Cats

Even seeing the same character on facing pages in two single-page illustrations can provoke this sort of confusion as children work to master the picture book as a sequential art form. Once when I was reading Ezra Jack Keats's *The Snowy Day*, a little boy looked at the spread illustrating Peter going up the snowy hill on the verso page and then sliding down the hill on the recto.

"Look! That boy's mother and father had another little boy!" he exclaimed.

His misperception was resolved when I turned his comment over to the group and another child said, "That's just Peter climbing the hill there and sliding down there."

"Oh, yeah," said the first little boy, and I could almost see the proverbial light bulb illuminate over his head.

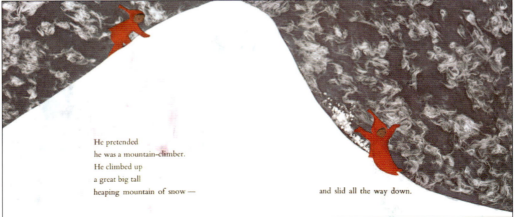

He pretended
he was a mountain-climber.
He climbed up
a great big tall
heaping mountain of snow —

and slid all the way down.

from *The Snowy Day*

While potential for confusion may arise in spreads such as these, opportunities for grasping how pictures communicate the passage of time with simultaneous succession abound. For example, an interior spread from I. C. Springman and Brian Lies's *More* features what could appear to be a whole flock of birds, but the intention in the narrative is to show one bird at many different moments in time, all compressed into a single spread. Taking the time to discuss this strategy invites children to understand the rich narrative potential of picture book art.

And yet, not all misperceptions in picture reading are easily resolved. Once, when I was reading *Come Along, Daisy!* by Jane Simmons with my then two-year-old daughter Emilia, she was stumped when Daisy and Mama Duck get separated. The picture shows Daisy in the foreground of the picture, looking large and lost, and Mama Duck in the background, looking small and distant. To Emilia, the picture presented a somewhat alarming upending of the relative sizes of mamas and babies.

"Mama tiny?" she asked, with her own tiny brow all furrowed. She then flipped back to a page with a different compositional perspective: Mama Duck in the foreground, with Daisy small beside her. "Mama big," she said contentedly.

from *Come Along, Daisy!*

As this mama explained to her daughter that Simmons was trying to depict characters as near or far from the reader, I had a double whammy of an epiphany: we adults shouldn't take children's visual perceptions for granted, and there's a big difference between reading a picture book and finishing a picture book. "Reading a picture book" implies reading words, pictures, and the design—the whole book—while "finishing a picture book" is focused on just reading through at the clip of the text, perhaps to beat the school bell or to get to bedtime. If I had simply moved forward in my reading of *Come Along, Daisy!* at the pace of the text, without pausing to talk with Emilia about the art and her confusion about it, I would

from Come Along, Daisy!

have missed a chance to help her grasp the principles and conventions of art that convey perspective. I don't think that Emilia fully mastered this concept during that conversation, but I do know that this particular incident was yet another experience in her ever-broadening repertoire of picture reading, supporting her developing visual literacy skills.

Another instance of Whole Book Approach conversation around aberrant picture reading (this one featuring not a mama but a daddy) occurred during a storytime at the Carle featuring Mo Willems's *Knuffle Bunny: A Cautionary Tale.*

"Why does she have so many arms?" asked a three-year-old child upon seeing a picture of Trixie having a fit while her clueless father looks on. I stifled a laugh as I looked at the picture myself and realized that instead of grasping the comic-art convention of repeated forms and motion lines conveying movement (in this case, the flailing arms of a temper tantrum), the storytime child thought Trixie was so distraught over her missing Knuffle Bunny that she'd sprouted new appendages in an impressive corporeal feat of outrage. I reflected on the notion that failing to allow space for children to clarify points of confusion could undermine their overall enjoyment or comprehension of a story—it's easy to see how a child could get distracted

She did everything she could to show how unhappy she was.

from Knuffle Bunny: A Cautionary Tale

from the progression of a story if he were stuck wondering about the sudden appearance, and then disappearance, of new arms. Instead of answering the child's question myself, I turned it over to the group to puzzle out.

"She doesn't have lots of arms. She's just waving one around because she's upset," explained another child, who was just a bit older. And then we all waved our hands in front of our faces to see how the movement created the visual illusion of many hands on one wrist. I'll say it again: children are learning to read pictures as surely as they are learning to read words, and providing them with the time and space to talk with one another about what they see can lead to richer picture book reading experiences for all of us.

Children are learning to read pictures as surely as they are learning to read words.

Chapter 8

The Picture Book Playground

The Benefits (and Fun) of the Whole Book Approach

Some of the most gratifying responses I've had to the Whole Book Approach have come from adults—teachers, librarians, and parents alike—who realize that implementing its techniques is eminently doable. The word "approach" is important here: as I noted in the preface, this isn't a curriculum or a prescriptive methodology in which certain questions must be asked in a certain order. Instead, it's an intentional, inquiry-based approach to reading aloud that puts art and design (and children's responses to them) at the center of the storytime experience. The educational philosophy behind it is constructivist and progressive: if we reject the outmoded way of thinking that says children should be seen and not heard, we can surely embrace children's voices at storytime as we encourage them to build their own knowledge and understanding.

Philip Yenawine advocates for progressive, constructivist educational approaches in his book *Visual Thinking Strategies: Using Art to Deepen Learning Across School Disciplines*, where he writes:

> *The remarkable cognition of which children are capable is almost taken for granted, and the fact of children's essential role in learning is little recognized either at home or at school. By the time kids are three, four, and five, both teachers and parents spend a lot of time telling them what to do, wear, eat, and learn. Adults read to young ones, quickly turning pages to follow the course of the written text and making only cursory reference to illustrations.*[35]

As I've noted in my reflections on my development of the Whole Book Approach, it took me a long time to really learn to slow down and stop quickly turning the pages in my own storytime practice, and learning about Visual Thinking Strategies played a key role in helping me to do so. Although the Whole Book Approach necessarily departs from VTS, which is used to look at individual works of art, VTS's techniques and questions have inspired and informed me tremendously as I've endeavored to make much more than cursory reference to illustrations—and design—at storytime.

When adults resist Whole Book Approach methods, it's often because they worry that stopping and starting the reading to talk about art and design holds the risk of explaining it to death, akin to explaining a joke and killing its humor. As essayist and children's book writer E. B. White famously said, "Humor can be dissected, as a frog can, but the thing dies in the process and the innards are discouraging to any but the pure scientific mind."[36] On the other hand, I've observed many, many children positively reveling in explaining jokes and hearing them explained—gaining as much pleasure from confirming their understanding of the humor as they do from the humor itself. Such conversation is both validating and promoting of inclusivity with its affirmation of being in the know.

That said, in Whole Book Approach storytimes, I certainly don't wish to undermine what some describe as ecstatic or aesthetic reading, which is when one reads for pleasure and becomes completely absorbed in a book, as opposed to critical or efferent reading, when one is more detached from the book in order to gain knowledge and engage in analysis.[37] Arthur Krystal expands on this juxtaposition in an essay from Anne Fadiman's edited collection *Rereadings: Seventeen Writers Revisit Books They Love*, saying:

> *Schooling and swooning don't mesh, and once we begin to differentiate the rhetorical devices that stylistically and thematically inform different narratives,*

the innocence, the thrill, and the trusting acceptance disappear. Replaced, to be sure, by the edifying feeling that one is learning something valuable. And of course, there is pleasure to be had from analysis, but it is a more complicated pleasure than giving oneself over completely to stories. However you slice it, reading critically is a more solemn affair than reading ecstatically.[38]

After thinking a lot about this, I've ended up questioning the presumed opposition between ecstatic and critical reading stances and Krystal's ultimate conclusion about reading critically as "a more solemn affair." I see my Whole Book Approach as fostering what might be called ecstatic criticism as I try to support children's engagement with the picture book as an art form. Much of this work simply involves getting out of children's way and slowing down the pace of the reading. This is accomplished in part by directing children's attention to paratexts, design, and illustration, and by seeing what these visual and material aspects of the book provoke in children as they merge what they see with what they hear by drawing upon prior knowledge and forming the composite text.

I think the key here is to keep the tone of the storytime *playful*—a word that I latched onto in 2010, when librarian Wendy Lukehart invited me to give a speech about the Whole Book Approach and my experiences reading aloud with children at the Association for Library Service to Children preconference "Drawn to Delight: How Picturebooks Work (and Play) Today," which she was organizing in Washington, DC. I was honored and delighted to participate, and my excitement only increased when Wendy delivered her opening remarks at the beginning of the day, excerpted in part below:

Why are we, children and adults alike, drawn to picturebooks? There are probably a host of reasons we could name—aesthetic, spiritual, pedagogic, nostalgic, and so on—but we Americans are somehow comforted by scientific explanations. In trying to find an authoritative discussion on this question, I came across a book by English scholar Brian Boyd, entitled On the Origin of Stories, *published in conjunction with Charles Darwin's anniversary. When I saw that he included an analysis of* Horton Hears a Who! *I read on.*

> **I see my Whole Book Approach as fostering what might be called ecstatic criticism as I try to support children's engagement with the picture book as an art form.**

At the risk of vast oversimplification, in Boyd's worldview, art is a human adaptation that derives from play. Art is to the mind of humans, what play is to the body of two- and four-legged creatures. Scientists note that as creatures play "repeatedly and exuberantly," they refine skills, sharpen sensitivities and tone muscles. In the process, they release dopamine—that neurotransmitter associated with pleasure that is a key motivator of behaviors that need to be repeated for survival, like eating—and other enjoyable behaviors that need to be repeated for survival. Play, therefore, has evolved to be highly self-rewarding.

Boyd explains that we humans gain most of our advantages from intelligence, so our appetite is for information, especially for pattern. . . . [He then] defines art as "cognitive play with pattern," and just as play refines behavior over time for animals, art increases cognitive skills and sensitivities in people, with similar neural responses and benefits. He asserts that a work of art acts like a "playground for the mind, a swing or a slide or a merry-go-round of visual or aural or social pattern."

I love the image of the picturebook as a cognitive playground. Can't you just imagine children's minds climbing gleefully up the monkey bars as they interact with an adult and a marvelous book? I think back to the first time, maybe fifteen years ago or so, when I saw the dramatic color differences in the brain scans comparing young children who had been read to and those who hadn't, and I'm intrigued by this explanation of the rewards of art.[39]

Reading picture books while using Whole Book Approach techniques and gleaning those "rewards of art" does feel tremendously playful. Little disheartens me more at storytime than a docile, silent group. Furthermore, no matter how raptly my own kids listen to books read aloud at home, I'd be surprised to experience a reading with them that was unpunctuated by their spontaneous reactions and questions. These experiences are also often characterized by playful, intertextual readings that revel in making connections between picture books, swinging from one book to the next like a child moving across monkey bars, with one hand grasping behind while the other swings ahead.

For example, back when my daughter Emilia was a young toddler, Eric Carle's *The Very Busy Spider* was one of her very favorite books. She was about eighteen months old at the time I introduced it to her, and I vividly recall her touching her tiny finger to the page and noticing the raised texture of the spider's body. She was fascinated. She ran her hand across the page and felt the web and the fly, also raised up off the page. She then touched the pictures of the farm animals and frowned a bit—they weren't textured like the other parts of the

illustrations. When we reached the end of the book, she said, "More," and so we read it again.

And again.

And again.

And again.

Over the next few weeks, I read that book with Emilia many times a day, and I began to understand why family lore has it that my parents hid my copy of *Green Eggs and Ham* from me when I was a toddler. I decided we needed to branch out into other Carle works, and so I brought home a copy of *The Very Quiet Cricket*. The first thing Emilia did when I opened up the book was run her hand over the page to see if there was a raised texture to the illustrations. I was amazed as I witnessed this very young child recognizing an artist's style. At eighteen months old, she had become familiar with materials, technique, palette, and style to the extent that she could look at a totally different book by a favorite artist and understand that he had created it, too.

This interaction reminded me of a story I heard years ago at a conference when biographer Ann Thwaite spoke about A. A. Milne, the author of the Winnie-the-Pooh books, illustrated by Ernest H. Shepard. Thwaite said that her grandchildren were great fans of the Pooh stories and that when one grandson was a toddler, he saw a Shepard illustration from an entirely different book hanging up in a bookstore—and delightedly said, "Pooh!"

"He's clearly a genius, don't you think?" she quipped with grandmotherly pride.[40]

Well, I admit that's exactly what I thought when Emilia made her Carle connection. But now I'm not so sure. Not to knock my daughter's or Thwaite's grandson's respective levels of genius, but many other experiences like these have shown me that the recognition of an artist's style is a skill that can develop very early on in many children and can afford them great pleasure in their interactions with and thinking about books.

In my professional life, a favorite example of children's ability to recognize art style comes from my outreach work on behalf of the Eric Carle Museum of Picture Book Art. I frequently read *Where the Wild Things Are* by Maurice Sendak. Many children are already familiar with the book, but I like to help them see it with new eyes through the Whole Book Approach, and one point of focus is the illustration immediately following the three wordless double-page spreads that comprise the wild rumpus. In this picture Max sits dejectedly in his tent on a three-legged stool, his chin resting

> **Recognition of an artist's style is a skill that can develop very early on.**

in his hand like Auguste Rodin's *The Thinker*. The text tells us, "And Max the king of all wild things was lonely and wanted to be where someone loved him best of all."

"His mom is who loves him like that," a little girl said.

"Yeah, and that wild thing with the long hair looks like his mom," added a classmate.

Now, Max's mother is never depicted in the book, so I was curious as to what made this child say such a thing. I suspected it was just an allegiance to gender norms that made this child think long hair equals female equals mom. But I asked anyway.

"What makes you say that wild thing looks like Max's mom?"

"The long, dark hair."

"So Max's mom has long, dark hair?"

"Yes. And a blue dress and an apron."

What fascinating specificity! This child had clearly filled in a gap in the visual storytelling with his own imagined vision of Max's mother. We carried on with the reading, and I thought nothing more of this interaction until a few months later, when, in a different school, a different child said to me, "That wild thing with the long, dark hair looks like Max's mother."

"Really?" I asked. And then I couldn't resist following up with "What does Max's mother look like?"

"She has long dark hair, and she wears a blue dress and an apron."

I was stumped. Was there some underground version of *Where the Wild Things' Mothers Are* that I had missed? Was there secret fan fiction depicting Max's mother in all her apron-clad glory? I puzzled over this for some time, and then one day the answer sang out to me—in the voice of Carole King.

"There once was a boy named Pierre, who only would say, 'I don't care.'"

My children love Maurice Sendak's *Nutshell Library* and the *Really Rosie* CD it inspired. We listen to it quite a bit, and one day I was singing along to "Pierre" with my son Stevie and daughter Caroline while looking at the book with them, and I saw her there: Pierre's mom. What do you know—she has long(ish), dark hair, and she wears a blue dress and an apron. Eureka! Pierre looks an awful lot like Max, so this must have been where my storytime attendees had found their image of Max's mother. The children weren't simply reiterating gender norms; they were drawing upon prior knowledge and exercising a sophisticated recognition of artistic style.

A similar experience arose in the aftermath of my service on the 2012 Boston Globe–Horn Book Award Committee. After we'd made our selections, I delighted in returning home and sharing the picture book winners with my children. "Those are the guys from that funny hat book!" Caroline exclaimed, pointing to the bear and bunny standing in line with a bevy of other characters for whom little Annabelle has knitted sweaters in Mac Barnett and Jon Klassen's *Extra Yarn*. Caroline was drawing a connection between it and Klassen's earlier solo title, *I Want My Hat Back*. Her sister and brother, Emilia and Stevie, were delighted by this insight and clamored for me to read "that funny hat book"—a title that had become a favorite as soon as I'd received it a few months prior. Emilia quickly found it, and when we got to the end, Caroline pointed to *Extra Yarn* and said, "So this book must've happened *before* the hat book did

> The children weren't simply reiterating gender norms; they were drawing upon prior knowledge and exercising a sophisticated recognition of artistic style.

from *Extra Yarn*

She made sweaters for all the dogs,

and all the cats,

and for other animals, too.

Soon, people thought, soon Annabelle will run out of yarn.

because the bunny isn't dead there." Ah, if only Annabelle had knitted the bunny a hat! Perhaps it could have avoided its sad fate in Klassen's tale of ursine revenge.

Caroline's delight in intertextuality fostered other book pairings in our shared reading, and one less obvious instance left me shaking my head in wonder at her precocious ability to bring one picture book into dialogue with another. We were reading Julie Fogliano and Erin Stead's *And Then It's Spring*, a Boston Globe–Horn Book Honor book, and I told Caroline that it made me think of Ruth Krauss and Crockett Johnson's *The Carrot Seed*. Others have compared Fogliano's lovely text to Krauss's understated, masterful picture book writing, and I saw thematic links as well, between Krauss's little boy's faith and hope in a carrot seed and Fogliano's broader depiction of a child's wait for spring. But Caroline, unconvinced, shook her head.

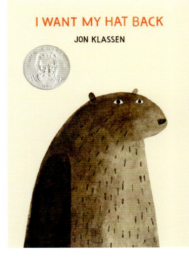

I WANT MY HAT BACK

JON KLASSEN

"No, that's not the carrot seed boy," she said, taking my comparison to mean that I thought this was the same child in both books, just as she'd seen the same bear and bunny in *I Want My Hat Back* and *Extra Yarn*. A moment later she continued, "But I know who that boy is!"

"Who?" I asked.

"That's Amos McGee when he was a little boy. See how he loves all those animals so much?"

She pointed to the little peaceable kingdom that accompanies Fogliano and Stead's boy through his hopeful wait for spring. Though they aren't the same zoo animal friends who surround Amos McGee on his sick day in Erin Stead's Caldecott Medal–winning title penned by her husband Philip C. Stead, I could see the connection Caroline was making. And she didn't stop there.

"And look, Mom-Mom," she continued, "he's wearing a blue jacket just like Amos does at the zoo. And see the boy's little house? Amos has a little house, too! It's him! I just know it's him!"

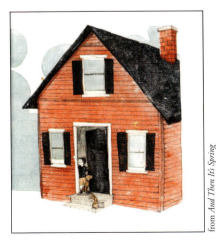

from *And Then It's Spring*

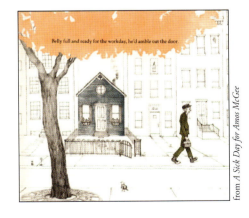

from *A Sick Day for Amos McGee*

I didn't have the heart to correct Caroline and remind her that Amos wears green, or to point out that the boy's little house in *And Then It's Spring* is red, while Amos's little house in the city is blue. Besides, I don't think such details really matter. Caroline was recognizing the books' shared color palette, as well as their shared artistic style, and she was just plain delighted about getting to know her friend Amos a little better by seeing him as a child. The sophistication of this insight left me a little breathless, and I immediately became impatient for the release of Erin Stead's next picture book so I could share it with my daughter.

The playfulness inherent in these storytime stories about children drawing connections between books embodies the spirit with which I strive to infuse every Whole Book Approach reading. Far from undermining the enjoyment of a picture book and rendering storytime "a more solemn affair," I've found that interactive, shared reading transactions focused on art and design enhance the pleasure of storytime because they position the picture book as a meeting space for child and adult. By slowing down the reading to accommodate and encourage discussion about paratexts, design and production elements, and illustration, the Whole Book Approach swings wide the gates to the picture book as a playground for the mind, affirming that the child's voice is crucial to the success of a dynamic and, yes, playful storytime experience.

The Story Continues

"Your epitaph will read, 'She made them look at endpapers,'" a parent attendee of storytime at the Carle once quipped.

Better than "Here Lies Storytime" or "The End," I decided—and truly, I can think of far lesser legacies. Endpapers, after all, are an important part of the codex picture book, and although there are many exciting things about developing ebook technologies and platforms, it probably goes without saying that I'm a codex devotee who'd be thrilled by such a summation of my professional accomplishments. Like so many others, I appreciate the ease and convenience of screen readers, but a Kindle can't hold a candle to the love I have for a book in hand. That's part of the reason why I approached an October

2010 *New York Times* article entitled "Picture Books No Longer a Staple for Children" with more than a little dismay. *Really*? I thought. *Says who*? I was serving on the 2011 Caldecott committee at the time and was up to my delighted eyeballs in brand-new picture books. Although my professional and personal contexts might have predisposed me to resist the premise of the article from the start, I wasn't alone. In a matter of hours, nearly four hundred people responded with online comments, and just about all of them engaged in what might be termed picture book apologetics, as they steadfastly rejected the notion that the picture book was dead or even just in the sickbed next to Madeline and her burst appendix.

While I resist some of the hand-wringing sentiment around such talk, I'm intrigued by how the field of children's literature is changing due to market and cultural forces, as well as the rise of new digital technologies. Amid these changes, and to underscore the ideas raised in the preface, I'd wager that far from dying or "no longer [being] a staple for children," the picture book will robustly outlast any other codex form due to its reliance on its physical bookness and how it creates a meeting space, that "playground for the mind," for children and adults to interact with one another on a common ground of words, pictures, and design. Indeed, as new digital-media forms evolve and books leave the page and head toward the screen, it seems as though there's also room for a parallel track of picture books that positively revel in their materiality and design and in the possibilities they hold for shared reading—and you can't really wring your hands if they're busy turning pages.

Although my own hands are no longer regularly turning pages at the Carle's storytimes, in 2014 I launched a two-credit course on the Whole Book Approach as a graduate elective at Simmons, and it's immensely gratifying that the Carle

You can't really wring your hands if they're busy turning pages.

continues to lead Whole Book Approach programs as a key part of its educational offerings. Regular storytimes are led there by volunteers and staff who are trained in the approach, and they generously welcome me to lead the occasional storytime in order to model Whole Book Approach techniques for my graduate students. The Carle's education department also continues to build on Whole Book Approach principles to offer trainings for teachers, librarians, and parents. Such work is helping to create more and more stories about how the Whole Book Approach engages kids, and it's been a pleasure to hear them recounted by colleagues, including my friend Emily Prabhaker, a graduate of Simmons and current educator at the Carle. When she visited my class to tell students about her work through the Carle, she also shared a story about her

Emily Prabhaker

then two-year-old daughter, Lucy, who puzzled over Pete the Cat's missing buttons in Eric Litwin and James Dean's *Pete the Cat and His Four Groovy Buttons.*

"Where the buttons go?" Lucy asked her mother.

Emily didn't have the answer, and so Lucy took matters into her own capable hands and flipped through the pages of her book in search of the missing buttons.

from *Pete the Cat and His Four Groovy Buttons*

"There they are! The bird has all the buttons!" Lucy exclaimed when she reached the copyright page. Emily looked to see a tiny vignette of a yellow bird perched on its nest, and lo and behold, in that nest were Pete's four groovy buttons.

If Lucy can find Pete's buttons, who knows what groovy things children will find in the picture books you read together during Whole Book Approach storytimes.

My hope is that the Whole Book Approach plays a role in examining the place the picture book can hold in the reading life of a child and in adult/child interactions when we meet in its pages, no matter the era or the *Times.* Consider the wisdom in the child's oft-stated demand to "read it again!" Perhaps the ideas I've raised here will encourage you to reread picture books you know and love with new eyes, or to discover new ones with even greater attention to the potential of the form and to making space for children's responses to it. As these collected Whole Book Approach anecdotes document, encouraging and listening to children talk about endpapers and other parts of picture book art and design crystallizes the difference between reading picture books *to* children and reading them *with* children.

I know from experience that the former practice can be richly rewarding, but I've found that interactivity is the best way to prevent feeling as if one's role as a storytime leader is tantamount to crowd control; instead, interactivity asserts the reader as a facilitator of the group's shared experience.

> **I've found that interactivity is the best way to prevent feeling as if one's role as a storytime leader is tantamount to crowd control.**

I was humbled and thrilled by how the *Horn Book Magazine*'s Lolly Robinson described my work leading storytime at the Carle during its grand-opening weekend in November 2002:

> *I wandered into the museum's small library to rest my feet and happened onto a storytime that tied together my most basic wishes in one child-friendly package. Megan Lambert . . . proved that children as young as two or three can be kept entertained by the details of picture book creation. While reading Eric Carle and Bill Martin Jr.'s* Brown Bear, Brown Bear, What Do You See? *to a large group of children of various ages, she managed to explain pacing of text and art, the basics of layout, and even book production (jacket, binding,*

gutter). She kept it interactive, and the kids were fasci-nated. And I, a former preschool teacher, had a feeling of satisfaction akin to hearing a sublimely performed concerto: I was witnessing a perfect group time.[41]

A "perfect group time"—huzzah! Leading Whole Book Approach storytimes really does feel like conducting an orchestra in some ways. Picture books are our score, and I read aloud and facilitate discussion, but the children who respond to the words, pictures, and design elements of the books are the ones making the meaning and making the metaphorical music together.

And what about those children? I've found that those who tend to have a harder time during traditional story-times seem to get a lot out of thinking visually, stopping and starting the narrative, and working with the group as a whole. The aural learners in the group, however, some-times are resistant. "Can't you just *reeeead* the book?!" I've heard on occasion.

"We *are* reading the book. We're reading the pictures, too," is my standard response.

I had a back-and-forth like this with a third grader during an outreach storytime on behalf of the Carle. She told me she'd already read *Where the Wild Things Are* "a million times" and was resist-

> **We *are* reading the book. We're reading the pictures, too.**

ant to my efforts to encourage her and her classmates to watch the air frames around the pictures. But as we moved forward with reading the book (its words, pictures, and yes, those changing air frames that direct the design of the pages), I started to see a light go on in her eyes.

"They're getting bigger!" she exclaimed after we'd turned a few pages to see the air frames diminish as the pictures take up more and more space on the verso page and then spill over onto the recto, culminating in the three full-bleed double-page spreads at the heart of the book before the white space returns and the pictures shrink in size.

When we reached the end of the book, I expectantly waited for her chagrined yet wondrous response. Surely she'd marvel at how attending to design had allowed her to kindle a new appreciation for this book she'd read "a million times"?

"The pictures don't do that in my book at home!" she reported, fascinated at this discovery but unable to believe that she'd missed such an integral part of the book's design in her millions of prior readings.

The Whole Book Approach is an opportunity to stretch her and others like her as learners. At the same time, the techniques I use foster success in students who typically have a harder time staying engaged with a reading that does not emphasize the visual elements of a picture book or promote discussion.

We spent the rest of that storytime talking about pictures breaking the page, and about how a frame around a picture on a page can make you feel like you're on the outside looking in, but a picture without a frame can make you feel like you are right inside the picture world—a participant rather than a spectator. And that's ultimately what

I want children to be in Whole Book Approach story-times: participants, rather than spectators—ecstatic critics engaging with all that picture books have to offer and de-lighting in what they hear *and* see.

Acknowledgments

I'm thankful to the Mass Literacy Champion Awards (www.massliteracy.org) for the funding to support my writing during the early stages of this book. I am also deeply grateful to the staff at the Eric Carle Museum of Picture Book Art, especially founding curator of education and senior educator Rosemary Agoglia, founding director and chief curator Nick Clark, and executive director Alix Kennedy, for providing me with such an inspiring professional home in which to develop my ideas. Thanks also to Eric and Barbara Carle, who had the dream and the vision necessary to create such a magnificent museum in the first place, and to the hundreds of people and organizations that have supported my work on the Whole Book Approach by inviting me to speak at conferences and meetings or by hosting visiting storytimes and professional development programs. Special thanks to DC Public Library superstar Wendy Lukehart, whose wonderful words about looking at art as cognitive play are included in this book. This entire book is a thank-you to the thousands of children whom I have read *with* over the years as we engaged in the cognitive play of Whole Book Approach storytimes.

I am deeply indebted to Anna Markus, former visiting lecturer at Smith College and Mount Holyoke College, who set me on my professional path in the first place and who remains a dear friend. Likewise, Cathryn Mercier, the director of the Center for the Study of Children's Literature at Simmons College, and my instructors in the program's picture book class, director emeritus Susan Bloom and instructor Michael Patrick Hearn, all provided me with an outstanding education in the field. I'm grateful every day for the ways that they've continued to support my efforts to teach others and to keep growing myself, and I cherish the relationships that have grown out of this work—especially the times I've shared with Susan and her husband, David Bloom. And although the word sounds rather cold given her extraordinary warmth toward me, I want to acknowledge that Cathie has been a remarkable boss at Simmons. She's championed my teaching and carried out an extraordinary vision for our program by following in the big footsteps of Susan's leadership. Simmons is a special place with remarkable people, and I'll always strive to give back as much as it's given me.

And because teaching is where I do my best learning, I am grateful to my students, whose commitment to their own learning inspires me to keep learning, too. Particular

Acknowledgments

thanks go to Siân Gaetano, who served as my research assistant for this project, and to Rebekah Dutkiewicz, whose independent study using the Whole Book Approach in her preschool classroom has allowed her to share new storytime stories about her students with my classes. I've also learned a tremendous amount from the fabulous team at Charlesbridge: editor extraordinaire Yolanda Scott, editorial team members Karen Boss and Julie Bliven, intern Russell Perry (who even took on the task of tackling the glossary), copyeditor Josette Haddad, and art director Susan Sherman. I am also deeply appreciative of attorney Debra Kass Orenstein's work on our contract, which enables me to give back to the Eric Carle Museum of Picture Book Art for its support of my work through some of the proceeds of this book.

Laura Vaccaro Seeger thrilled me to my toes when she agreed to create the cover art for the book. Her remarkable picture books are an inspiration to me and are among the best of the form. I was humbled by her acceptance of this project. Likewise, I am delighted by Chris Raschka's foreword. When we shared the stage as panelists at the American Library Association's annual conference in 2013, I knew I wanted Chris to contribute. I am so pleased that he said yes and then said so much more in his thoughtful comments. Thanks to all the artists and publishers who gave permission for me to include their artwork in this book, with special thanks to those who waived their typical fee in recognition of this project's support of the Eric Carle Museum of Picture Book Art.

I'd also like to thank my family and friends and all those who've helped me balance life as a mother, writer, and teacher. I once heard author/professor/mother-of-five Donna Jo Napoli quip, "When people ask me, 'How do you do it all?' I respond: 'Badly. You could eat off my kitchen floor . . . for weeks.'" So even though we don't know each other, thanks to Donna Jo for that sentiment, which makes me feel better about myself and my kitchen floor every single day. Thanks also to my children, Rory, Natayja, Emilia, Stevie, and Caroline, for all our times reading together and for all the times when I asked you to wait just one minute so I could finish writing something; to their outstanding teachers in the Amherst Regional Public Schools; to their other mom, Dana Mergendahl, for her excellent co-parenting of our crew, and to her partner, Ramsey Kurdi; to my own mom, Linda Dowd Lambert, for *her* excellent parenting and grandparenting—especially during final grading periods; to my dad, Ray Lambert, for his loving support and for reading an early version of the manuscript and cheering me on; to my siblings, Sean and Keita Lambert, for contributing so meaningfully to the story of my own life; to my nephew and niece, Ezrah and Sasha Lambert, for their special place in our family, especially as my children's cousins; to my cousin, Kevin Lambert, and his wife, Theresa Schwegel, fellow writers and book lovers who were readers of the manuscript as I tried to title it, and whose emails and letters mean more than they'll ever know; and to all of the St. Maries—Ann and Terry, Brian and Laurie, Chrissy, Sienna,

Acknowledgments

Bradyn, and Liam—for their warm embrace of all of us Lamberts; and to Michael and Megan Lewis-Schurter and their son, Tristan; Ali Wicks-Lim, Emily Prabhaker, David Hyde Costello, Laurie Flynn, Vicky Smith, Hilary Price, Katja Guenther, Kate Nicolaou, Kate Manning, and Bronwen Exter—kindred spirits, all.

Finally, thanks to my husband and best reader, Sean P. Lambert St. Marie. Now that our new baby, Jesse, is here we'll have so many opportunites to read picture books *with* him, too.

Leading Whole Book Approach Storytimes

Now that you've read this book and reflected on ideas about reading picture books with children, where to begin? Here are some of the questions that teachers, parents, and librarians have asked me over the years.

How do I begin leading Whole Book Approach storytimes?

During your independent reading of picture books, keep the Whole Book Approach in mind. You'll probably find certain elements of each book that stand out as particularly successful or problematic. You might anticipate that a group sharing a particular picture book during storytime will make similar observations, but your primary role is to open up the potential for making meaning, not to lead participants toward a certain idea. As children consider a picture book's art and design while you read the text out loud to them, you should intentionally attend to the different parts of the book—mention design, production, and art vocabulary in order to give children the verbal tools to talk about what they see. Many of the children's responses in this book were provoked when I simply pointed out a part of the book and asked kids to pay attention to it as I read aloud.

For example, when reading *Where the Wild Things Are*, I might say: "This white space around the picture is called an air frame. Watch the air frame as I turn the pages, and tell me what you see."

Or I've said, "Take a look at the gutter in this picture," while looking at the front-matter illustration in *Yo! Yes?* by Chris Raschka, and then asked, "What do you see happening in this picture as you think about the gutter?"

"The two boys are separated," comes the response.

So I follow up with: "OK, now watch the gutter as I read the book aloud, and let me know what you notice."

And so on.

As you make sure to note the different parts of the picture book, pay attention to children's spontaneous reactions to art, design, and story, and then weave them into the shared reading experience that you're creating with the group.

What if I have a very quiet group?

Keep in mind that while children often verbalize their responses as questions, exclamations, or statements, some responses may be nonverbal. For example, children often mimic the facial expressions that they see in illustrations, especially when strong emotions are depicted. Taking the time to point out children's physical engagement with the art can lead to a deeper discussion with a group.

"Why are you making such an angry face?" I've asked when I've seen children mirror Sophie's scowl in *When Sophie Gets Angry—Really, Really Angry . . .* by Molly Bang.

"Because she looks so angry!"

"What do you see that makes you say that?" I might then say, prompting them to reflect not only on how and why her face looks angry, but perhaps on the red of the background color, or the way the close-up of her face makes her seem like she's, well, in your face.

If you're reading with a particularly quiet group or child, ask open-ended questions to prompt discussion about the art, design, and story. The Visual Thinking Strategies questions (What's going on in this picture? What do you see that makes you say that? What more can we find?) and questions designed to draw attention to a particular design or art element are good possibilities. Or you could reassess your goals for the shared reading. There's nothing wrong with switching gears to a story-telling or performance mode if that's what children need and want.

How do you keep kids on topic?

I respond to this concern by reflecting on what I call "I have a dog" responses to pictures. Literacy experts and reader-response theorists discuss various ways that children draw upon their schemas—their respective repertoires of life and reading experiences—to make meaning of texts. Ellin Oliver Keene and Susan Zimmermann found that comprehension improves when readers make different kinds of connections: text to self, text to text, and text to world.[42] And yet, the impulse toward text-to-self connections, especially, can lead to a lot of "I have a dog" statements that risk pulling attention away from a reading. This is of particular concern in Whole Book Approach storytimes, since children have been encouraged to pipe up with responses to art and design. So, as those "I have a dog" comments start to come fast and furiously, I try to identify a child who's been on the quiet side, and first validate her response and then redirect it back to the picture. I might say, for example:

"Wow. Lots of you have dogs or know dogs. Erin, I haven't heard much from you yet today, but I heard you say that you have a dog. Is your dog white like the one on this page?"

In the end, the picture book is the common ground that the group shares, whether they all have dogs, or someone's grandma has a dog, or someone is allergic to dogs. No matter what might get a group off topic, using validation and redirection to bring the group back to the picture at hand is the name of the game.

How do you keep things moving?

As I remarked earlier, there is a big difference between reading a picture book and finishing a picture book, so I try to be mindful of not rushing. There are times, however, when I feel like I'm starting to lose part of the group as the rest of the kids clamor to share their insights about endpapers, framing, or some other element of illustration or design. When I see this happening, I don't want to indulge the more talkative children at the expense of those who are drifting, but I also don't want to shut down or invalidate engagement. One way I move things along is centered on inclusivity, validation, and redirection, and makes the most of what Barbara Bader calls "the drama of the turning of the page."[43] I call it the "one-two-three page turn," and it goes something like this:

"We've had so many interesting things to say about this picture, but I think we're ready to see what's going to happen next. Everyone count to three with me and we'll turn the page."

One, two, three—magic.

This technique allows the group to have agency to move to the next page instead of relegating me to the role of the shushing librarian.

And speaking of shushing, when children speak over one another, have side conversations, or in other ways lose focus or get noisy, inviting them to "count to three and make a quiet sound with me" is another way to gel the group while dealing with the problem. "One, two, three: *shhhhhhh*," we say together. This is much better than shushing the group myself, which could inadvertently shame those who were talking out of turn and potentially alienate kids from the conversation. This technique works especially well when I can relate "the quiet sound" to something happening in the story:

"Oh look, the bunny in this picture is in bed and wants to go to sleep. Let's count to three and make a quiet sound; then we'll turn the page and see if he is asleep. One, two, three: *shhhhh*."

How do you prevent talkative children from dominating the conversation?

There are a couple of different ways I address this concern. I always try to remember that some people figure out what they think by talking through their ideas and questions, while others are internal processors who figure out what they think before they speak up. It's important to give time and space to both kinds of learners in a discussion, but it's easy for the latter group to get lost in the shuffle. So I make a point of validating the role of listener by saying something like, "What a great job Alex is doing listening to everyone's comments." This sort of statement both validates the listener and invites chattier members of the group to open up their ears.

Or, after finishing one book and before moving on to another, I might say, "I noticed that a lot of you were really good listeners during our last reading. Thanks so much for that—we need good listeners to have good conversations." I heard the former curator of education at the Eric Carle Museum of Picture Book Art, Rosemary Agoglia, say something like this countless times in her Visual Thinking Strategies work in the galleries at the museum, and it always struck me (as a talker through and through) as a lovely way to support quieter people while reminding loquacious learners to strike a balance between speaking up and listening.

During a reading I might also say something to the effect of "Is there anyone who has not spoken yet who would like to share an idea? Who has a question?"

Or if I see a quiet child raise her hand alongside a more talkative one, I might say, "Sam, I have heard so many good ideas from you already, and I think your comments and questions made Carrie raise her hand. Let's see what she wants to say."

Does the story get lost in all the conversation about art and design?

This is probably the most common concern I hear. Many adults worry that the Whole Book Approach's attention to art and design might end up feeling about as rewarding as explaining why a joke is funny. This is definitely not the result I'm after, so I work to strike a balance between stopping and starting for comments and questions and progressing through the book. The main strategy I employ is to let children's spontaneous reactions drive the pace of the storytime so the picture book as an art form can provoke discussion. I do prompt groups with open-ended questions or with directives to consider particular design elements, but if the children in a group aren't interested in talking about, say, endpapers, or if they ask questions or make comments about other parts of the book, I try to follow their lead and facilitate the discussion that emerges. In this way, I avoid forced discussions and instead create a playful, organic outgrowth of the reading.

Whole Book Approach Sample Questions

The following questions are organized by chapter and are designed to both immerse you in the Whole Book Approach and to expand your understanding of it. Some of the questions are meant for you, as the leader of a storytime, to mull over. Others are questions you might ask children during storytime readings to better involve them in the whole book. I hope that these questions will help you develop your own personal Whole Book Approach flair for your storytimes—at home, at school, in the library, or in any other places where you meet with children in the pages of a picture book. Don't regard this as a script to follow; just dive in however you'd like to. You might begin with the endpapers, as I did, or perhaps you'll go right to a little gutter talk. Just remember to keep things playful.

Preface • Reading ~~to~~ *with* Children
Introduction • **How I Learned to Think with My Eyes**

In these opening sections of the book, I dig into my own learning and thinking about the picture book as a visual art form and how I share picture books with children. I invite you to do the same by reflecting on the following questions:

- *Do you tend to use a performance or a co-constructive storytime approach in your reading with children? What are the benefits for children? How could you enhance your practice?*

- *What are your typical goals when you read with children? How does your current approach help you meet them? How could you shake things up to better reach your goals or even create new ones?*

- *Can you think of times when children at storytime have noticed or commented on things you hadn't considered before? How might children's observations point you toward new ways of reading aloud and doing even more to welcome children's insights into your storytime practice?*

- *How comfortable are you when it comes to thinking with your eyes? Do you tend to privilege text in your reading of picture books? If so, what do you think might be gained by deeper attention to art and design?*

Chapter 1 • That's About the Size of It
Trim Size and Orientation

As I note in this chapter, I often like to juxtapose two books with contrasting portrait and landscape formats, holding them up together in front of the group. Then I ask:

- *Why do you think this book is so tall in a portrait format, and this one is long in a landscape format?*

This is a great way to jump-start visual thinking at the beginning of storytime. When a book adopts a square format, I might ask:

- *How would you describe a square?*

- *What sort of feeling does a square give you when you look at it?*

- *If a landscape book makes you feel like you're going on a journey, and a portrait one makes you feel like you're reaching up or diving down, what does a square do?*

- *What does the square shape of this picture book make you notice about the art?*

Just as comparing formats can create a leaning-in effect at the beginning of storytime, so too can juxtaposing two books with contrasting sizes. Holding them up together in front of the group, I ask:

• *Why do you think this book is so big and this one is so small?*

Give this question a try when you start a storytime. Doing so will welcome children to reflect on a basic element of book design, which will assure them that their small voices make a big difference in your reading.

Chapter 2 • Coming Attractions
Jackets and Covers

I often tell my students who are aspiring teachers or youth-services librarians that one of the best ways to improve our skills is to reposition ourselves as students in ways big and small. When my students struggle with something, I encourage them to think about how the struggle will inform their efforts to help a student in a future classroom, for example. The experience of trying something new or feeling as though you don't quite get something is an exercise in empathy with a young learner. This vein of thinking is also useful for veteran educators, librarians, and parents, since we all try to nurture children's growth and development in various ways.

So, as you approach your consideration of picture book jackets and covers, take a moment to situate yourself in the place of learning, discovery, and risk-taking that we adults ask children to occupy on a daily basis. Slow down and look at a picture book that has a dual-image jacket—a jacket with one picture on the front and another on the back, like the jacket from Allen Say's *Grandfather's Journey*. What connections can you make between the two images? How can you bring the pictures into dialogue with one another as you consider their presentation on the book jacket?

When evaluating the importance of good jacket design in the picture book form, here are questions to consider using during storytime:

- *Use Visual Thinking Strategies questions: What's going on in this picture? What do you see that makes you say that? What more can we find?*

- *For wraparound jacket art: Let's look first only at the front, and then open the book up to see the whole wraparound picture. Why do you think wraparound art works well for this book? What do you discover when you see the part of the picture that's on the back cover?*

- *For dual-image art: Look, there's one picture on the front of the jacket and another one on the back. Can you make connections between them?*

- *How does the jacket seem like a poster for the book, pulling us in as readers? What grabs your attention here?*

- *What information does the jacket give us about the story?*

• *What questions do you have after looking at these pictures?*

• *After reading the book, you might revisit the jacket and ask: How does this image (or these images) represent the book as a whole?*

If you're able to remove a picture book jacket during storytime, definitely do so in order to support children in exploring the whole book's design. If the jacket art is merely replicated on the casing, note this to the group. But if it's not, take the time to consider what new information or delights might be found on the casing. Questions to specifically ask about clothbound covers might include:

• *Why do you think the boards are this color? Can you make a color connection to the jacket art?*

• *What do you see in the blind-stamped (or foil-stamped, or ink-stamped) cover boards? Why do you think this image is important?*

Chapter 3 • Visual Overtures
Endpapers

Don't forget the endpapers! Often, readers are accustomed to at least glancing at jacket art, or pausing at front-matter pages, but endpapers get short shrift. Likewise, children are frequently familiar with the terms "jacket," "cover," and "title page," but "endpapers" might be a new word for them. So introduce it and invite them to read the endpaper design along with you by using some of the following questions:

- *Endpapers often give us clues about the story that a picture book tells. What clues do you see here?*

- *If the endpapers are a solid color, you can ask: Can you make a color connection between the endpapers and the jacket art?*

- *If the endpapers include a full illustration, try using Visual Thinking Strategies questions: What's going on in this picture? What do you see that makes you say that? What more can we find?*

Chapter 4 • Slow Down and Look
Front Matter

Attending to how front-matter pages ease readers into the book (or fail to do so) can inspire thoughtful reflection on the picture book form and its Walter Cranian architecture. While I often read basic written information from these pages (title, author and illustrator names, and even the publisher), I tend to focus on inviting children to make meaning of front-matter illustrations by using Visual

Thinking Strategies questions and referencing the specific names of the pages. This step can continue to set the stage for their visual engagement with the whole book:

- *What's going on in the picture on the title/copyright/ dedication page?*

- *What do you see that makes you say that?*

- *What more can we find?*

You might expand on these questions and ask children to connect their observations back to their reflections on the jacket, cover, or endpaper art. It's very likely they'll do this on their own once you've established that your story-time is a place where their insights matter and where connections are cause for celebration.

Chapter 5 • Knocked Out by Type
Typography

The printed text on a page conveys meaning not only through the definitions of the words themselves, but also through the visual appearance of those words with regard to typographic choices, such as typeface, size, weight, placement, and so on.

As I note in this chapter, sometimes I simply change the volume or tone of my voice to contradict the implied tone of the printed text itself—I might whisper words that appear very large on the page—and see how children react. Other times I ask more specific questions, such as:

- *How does the way the words look tell us how to read the words aloud?*

- *How would you describe what the words and letters look like on this page?*

- *Why do you think the words look like this on the page?*

While conventional wisdom has held that good typography recedes in order to allow design to support content, I'm intrigued by a shift toward considering how typographic design can serve as content in and of itself. Given how children have responded not only to the meanings of words read aloud but also to the meanings implied by what words look like, I am eager to do more investigation of this area, and I hope you are, too.

Chapter 6 • Gutter Talk and More
Page Design

The work you do to get kids talking about picture book paratexts before you start reading a story aloud can set the stage for their ongoing co-constructive participation in storytime. Consider using these questions to keep things flowing and to get kids talking about page layout:

- *Tell me why you think some pictures are framed and some bleed off the edge of the pages.*

- *Watch the framing in this picture book and tell me what you think about the artist's choices.*

- *Look at how the artist makes sure that nothing important in the pictures falls in the gutter of her book. What choices does she make to accomplish this?*

- *Look at how the gutter divides up the picture. Tell me why you think the artist made the choice to have some parts on the verso page and other parts on the recto page.*

Emphasizing that reading pictures is a part of reading picture books affirms the participation of children who can't yet read words, and also supports the visual literacy development of everyone in the group.

Chapter 7 • "Children, Children, What Do You See?"
Nurturing Visual Intelligence

In this chapter I document aberrant readings that arise when children misread elements of picture book art. With

Visual Thinking Strategies questions and techniques in mind, consider using the following questions if faced with an aberrant reading:

- *What do you see that makes you say that?*

- *Can anyone else tell me more about this picture?*

- *Does anyone else have a different idea about this picture?*

You might also use these questions to help children dig deeper into insights that surprise or intrigue you. The idea is to engage the group in ways that guide, as opposed to direct, the group's reading. Although the Whole Book Approach does not use VTS questions to examine every illustration in a book, acting as a facilitator (rather than as a storyteller) corresponds well with the way VTS is used to look at art in a museum. Whole Book Approach storytimes use many VTS discussion facilitation techniques, including:

- *Asking VTS questions and other open-ended questions to sup-port an inquiry-based engagement with art, design, and text.*

- *Paraphrasing responses to check for clarity, demonstrate active listening, and embed art, design, and literature-related vocabulary into the reading.*

- *Pointing to parts of the picture and book that children reference in their responses.*

- *Working to create an environment in which everyone is welcome to speak.*

The typical VTS session with one image or art object in a gallery lasts about twenty minutes. Because the Whole Book Approach is centered not on one image but on a whole book, the reader must work to strike a balance between moving through the reading of the text and stopping and starting to facilitate the group's discussion. Refer to the strategies mentioned on pages 108–115 as you prepare for and lead Whole Book Approach story-times:

- *Validation and redirection for "I have a dog" moments.*

- *One-two-three page turns.*

- *All-together quiet sounds: "One, two, three:* shhhhh.*"*

- *Remember that some children are external processers (big talkers) while others are internal processors (listeners), and make room for both kinds of engagement in your storytimes.*

- *Validate and invite active listening.*

Chapter 8 • **The Picture Book Playground**
The Benefits (and Fun) of the Whole Book Approach
Conclusion • **The Story Continues**

So how do you keep it playful? First and foremost, try to let children's responses, rather than your own agenda, set the pace of storytimes as you read aloud and facilitate discussion about the picture book as a visual art form. As you do so, keep in mind that we tend to expect children to behave very differently during storytimes at schools or libraries than we do when they're reading at home, and try to bridge that gap to keep things playfully interactive. Encourage intertextual connections, where children relate their reading of one book to their experiences with other books, as you bolster their sense of identity as readers and as thinkers about books and art. Then consider:

- *What anecdotes do you have from your storytime practice that document children making such connections?*

- *How might you develop your storytime practice to generate even more insights and connections from children?*

- *What do you think the codex picture book form offers children in today's digital environment?*

- *Finally, what do you learn about yourself as a reader and as a thinker when you reflect on your storytime experiences?*

Glossary of Book and Storytime Terminology

aberrant reading: A misreading (or nonstandard reading) of text or art.

air frame: White space or margins that surround a picture, in place of a frame defined by lines or decorative elements.

back matter: Pages within a bound book that are situated after the last page of the main text, or book proper.

binding: The fabric, glue, and/or stitching that holds the pages of a book together. Also a term that refers to the type of book: hardcover, paperback, board book, etc.

blind stamp: An unembellished, stamped impression on the casing of a book.

casing: The covering surrounding the boards of a hardcover book, most often made of paper or cloth.

co-constructive storytime: An interactive reading in which adult readers and children engage in extended, cognitively challenging conversation during the reading of a book.

codex: The physical object of a book, made of printed pages bound along one side within a cover.

copyright page: A page (usually located near the beginning of a book) that features the copyright and publication information, including the creator(s), publisher, year, and (for US books) Library of Congress cataloging data.

cover board: The cardboard foundation of a hardcover book, with bound pages inside. Front and back boards meet at the spine, and they are usually covered with a paper or cloth casing.

decorative framing: Illustrative or design embellishments that create a frame around a featured illustration or text block.

dedication page: The page (usually located near the beginning of a book) that features dedications from the author and/or illustrator.

dialogic reading: An interactive storytime model developed by Grover J. Whitehurst that uses a technique called the PEER sequence, in which the adult takes the following steps: **P**rompts the child to say something about the book, **E**valuates the child's response, **E**xpands the child's response by rephrasing and adding information to it, and **R**epeats the prompt to make sure the child has learned from the expansion.

double-page spread: Also called a double-spread, this is an illustration that crosses the gutter and takes up both pages of a book.

endpapers: Also called endsheets, these pages are glued to the inside of the boards of a hardcover book.

facing pages: The verso (left) and recto (right) pages of the same page opening, joined at the gutter by the binding.

flap: The end of a book jacket that folds over the inside of a book's cover and usually features information about the book (on the front flap) and information about the author and/or illustrator (on the back flap).

foil stamp: A stamped impression on a book's casing, filled in with foil.

frontispiece: A front-matter verso illustration that faces the title page. Found mostly in novels, but occasionally in picture books.

front matter: Pages within a bound book that are situated before the pages of the main text, such as the frontispiece, half-title page, title page, and dedication page.

full-bleed: An illustration that extends to all the edges of a page. May be either a single page or a double-page spread.

Glossary of Book and Storytime Terminolgy

gutter: The vertical seam between the verso (left) and recto (right) pages, where the pages are bound together.

half-title page: A front-matter page that typically displays only the title without a byline, subtitle, or other publishing information. It is sometimes anachronistically called "the bastard title."

ink stamp: A stamped impression on a book's casing, filled in with ink.

intertextual reading: A mode of reading in which readers derive meaning from their perceptions about the interdependent ways in which texts (including illustrated texts) stand in relation to each other.

intraiconic: Describes a non-illustrative element that serves as an integral part of a picture. This term is usually used to describe text depicted within an illustration.

jacket: Also called a book jacket or a dust jacket, this is the protective and decorative paper covering that fits over the casing of a hardcover book.

knockout type: Also called reversed type, this is white type on a dark-colored background.

landscape orientation: A horizontal layout for a book, with a shorter height than width.

loose-back Smyth-sewn binding: A special type of binding that allows a book to lie flat when opened and prevents artwork and text from becoming lost or unable to be seen in the gutter between the facing pages.

metafictive content: Material within a work of fiction that draws attention to its artificial (literary or artistic) nature, often by referring to itself.

metatextual content: Text that refers to another text.

multimodal text: A text that communicates through more than one semiotic mode, such as visual and verbal.

negative space: Areas that are unoccupied by objects in a picture and that help to define the illustration boundaries.

page opening: The two-page spread formed when a book is laid open to reveal facing pages joined at the gutter.

paratexts: The material of a book beyond the art and text of the main text, or book proper, such as the cover, jacket, endpapers, frontispiece, title page, and dedication page. These are sometimes referred to as peritexts, as in the work of Gérard Genette. In Genette's work, "paratexts" is then used as an umbrella term encompassing both the peritext and the epitext (material outside of a particular book that can impact its reading, such as publisher catalog copy or reviews of the book). Thus, paratext equals the peritext plus the epitext.

picture plane: The two-dimensional plane created by the surface of a printed page within a bound book.

portrait orientation: A vertical layout for a book, with a taller height than width.

recto: A right-hand page of a book.

sans serif: A typeface without protrusions, called serifs, that extend beyond the edge of the lines making up the characters (letters, numerals, and symbols).

serif: A typeface with protrusions, called serifs, that extend beyond the edge of the lines making up the characters (letters, numerals, and symbols).

shaped format: Any book printed and bound as something other than a square or rectangle.

simultaneous succession: Also called continuous narrative, this is a sequence of multiple pictures of the same figure(s) within a single page opening so that the changes from one image to the next convey the passage of time.

spine: The bound side of a book's cover that encloses the inner side of the pages and that faces outward when the book is shelved, typically displaying the title, and the names of the author, illustrator, and publisher.

spot art: A small, free-floating illustration that is usually a motif without a background.

title page: The front-matter page that displays the title, author, illustrator, and publisher of a book.

Glossary of Book and Storytime Terminolgy

trim size: The physical dimensions of the pages (not the cover dimensions) of a finished, bound book.

typeface: The specific design style that gives characters (letters, numerals, and symbols) their shape.

verso: A left-hand page of a book.

vignette: An illustration with either a faded or loosely defined border.

Visual Thinking Strategies (VTS): An inquiry-based education method developed by Abigail Housen and Philip Yenawine that is initiated by teacher-facilitated discussions of art images.

wordless spread: A spread that contains an illustration without any accompanying text.

Further Reading

Bader, Barbara. *American Picturebooks from Noah's Ark to The Beast Within*. New York: Macmillan, 1976.

Bang, Molly. *Picture This: How Pictures Work*. San Francisco: Chronicle Books, 2000.

Boog, Jason. *Born Reading: Bringing Up Bookworms in a Digital Age—From Picture Books to eBooks and Everything in Between*. New York: Touchstone, 2014.

Doonan, Jane. *Looking at Pictures in Picture Books*. Stroud, UK: Thimble Press, 1993.

Do Rozario, Rebecca-Anne C. "Consuming Books: Synergies of Materiality and Narrative in Picturebooks." *Children's Literature* 40 (2012): 151–66.

Fox, Mem. *Reading Magic: Why Reading Aloud to Our Children Will Change Their Lives Forever*, 2nd ed. (New York: Mariner, 2008).

Hammond, Heidi K., and Gail D. Nordstrom. *Reading the Art in Caldecott Award Books: A Guide to the Illustrations*. Lanham, MD: Rowman & Littlefield, 2014.

Harris, Pauline. "At the Interface Between Reader and Text: Devices in Children's Picturebooks that Mediate Reader Expectations and Interpretations." Paper presented at the Annual Conference of the Australian Association for Research in Education, Parramatta, Australia, November 2005.

Higgins, Carter. *Design of the Picture Book* (blog). www.designofthe picturebook.com/.

Horning, Kathleen T. *From Cover to Cover: Evaluating and Reviewing Children's Books*. Rev. ed. New York: HarperCollins, 2010.

Housen, Abigail, and Philip Yenawine. "Visual Thinking Strategies." www.vtshome.org.

Kiefer, Barbara Z. *The Potential of Picturebooks: From Visual Literacy to Aesthetic Understanding*. Englewood Cliffs, NJ: Merrill/ Prentice Hall, 1995.

Kümmerling-Meibauer, Bettina. *Picturebooks: Representation and Narration*. New York: Routledge, 2014.

Lambert, Megan. "Dave the Potter and Stevie the Reader." *Horn Book Magazine* (July/August 2011): 106–11.

———. "2012 BGHB Books in My Home." *Horn Book Magazine* (January/February 2013): 52–57.

———. "Gutter Talk and More: Picturebook Paratexts, Illustration, and Design at Storytime." *Children & Libraries: The Journal of the Association for Library Service to Children* 8, no. 3 (2010): 36–42, 46.

———. "Of Brown Bears and Mice and Picture Books: Reading Words and Pictures with Children." The Public Humanist, *Valley Advocate*, September 22, 2008. http://www.valleyadvocate.com /2008/09/22/of-brown-bears-and-mice-and-picture-books-read-ing-words-and-pictures-with-children.

———. "InFORMed Reading: Evaluating and Using Picture Books, Beginning Reader Books, and Illustrated Books." *Children & Libraries: The Journal of the Association for Library Service to Children* 4, no. 3 (2006): 31–54.

Lukehart, Wendy. "Art in Theory and Practice." *School Library Journal* 56, no. 1 (2010): 18–19.

————. "Art in Theory and Practice, II: How Do a Museum's Philosophies Work in a Public Library Setting?" *School Library Journal* 56, no. 2 (2010): 20–21.

————. "Playgrounds for the Mind: Drawn to Delight: How Picturebooks Work (and Play) Today." *Children & Libraries: The Journal of the Association for Library Service to Children* 8, no. 3 (2010): 32–35.

Marcus, Leonard S. *Show Me a Story!: Why Picture Books Matter: Conversations with 21 of the World's Most Celebrated Illustrators.* Somerville, MA: Candlewick Press, 2012.

————. *Ways of Telling: Conversations on the Art of the Picture Book.* New York: Dutton Children's Books, 2002.

————. "Give 'Em Helvetica: Picture Book Type," *Horn Book Magazine* (September/October 2012): 40–45.

Matulka, Denise I. *Picturing Books* (blog). http://www.picturing books.com.

Moebius, William. "Introduction to Picturebook Codes." *Word & Image: A Journal of Verbal/Visual Enquiry* 2 (April/June 1986): 141–58.

Nikolajeva, Maria, and Carole Scott. *How Picturebooks Work.* London: Routledge, 2000.

Nodelman, Perry. *Words About Pictures: The Narrative Art of Children's Picture Books.* Athens, GA: University of Georgia Press, 1988.

————. "Decoding the Images: How Picture Books Work." In *Understanding Children's Literature* 2nd ed., edited by Peter Hunt, 128–139. London: Routledge, 2005.

Nodelman, Perry, and Mavis Reimer. *The Pleasures of Children's Literature.* 3rd ed. New York: Pearson, 2002.

op de Beeck, Nathalie. *Suspended Animation: Children's Picture Books and the Fairy Tale of Modernity.* Minneapolis: University of Minnesota Press, 2010.

Raschka, Chris. "32 Pages and a Chipmunk; Or, What Is Appropriate Art for Children?" *Book Links* 7, no. 4 (March 1998): 33–37.

Further Reading

Robinson, Lolly. "What Do You See?: The Eric Carle Museum of Picture Book Art." *Horn Book Magazine* (May/June 2003): 317–323.

Roxburgh, Stephen. "The e-Future." *Horn Book Magazine* (March/April 2012): 10–21.

Scieszka, Jon, and Molly Leach. "Design Matters." *Horn Book Magazine* (March/April 2014): 28–40.

Serafini, Frank. *Reading the Visual: An Introduction to Teaching Multimodal Literacy*. New York: Teachers College Press, 2013.

Serafini, Frank, and Jennifer Clausen. "Typography as Semiotic Resource." *Journal of Visual Literacy* 31, no. 2 (2012): 2–16.

Shulevitz, Uri. *Writing with Pictures: How to Write and Illustrate Children's Books*. New York: Watson-Guptill, 1985.

Sutton, Roger, and Martha V. Parravano. *A Family of Readers: The Book Lover's Guide to Children's and Young Adult Literature*. Somerville, MA: Candlewick Press, 2010.

Yenawine, Philip. *Visual Thinking Strategies: Using Art to Deepen Learning Across School Disciplines*. Cambridge, MA: Harvard Education Press, 2013.

Notes

Preface

1 Sarah Ellis, "Opening Remarks for Dialogue III: Shaping Characters in Art and Text" (presentation, The Horn Book at Simmons Colloquium: Building Character, Boston, MA, October 5, 2013).

2 James Monaco, *How to Read a Film: Movies, Media, Multimedia*, 3rd ed. (1977; New York: Oxford University Press, 2000), 15.

3 Aidan Chambers, *Introducing Books to Children*, 2nd ed. (1973; Boston: *Horn Book Magazine*, 1983), 174–75.

Introduction

4 Walter Crane, *Of the Decorative Illustration of Books Old and New*, 3rd ed. (1896; London: George Bell and Sons, 1905), 184.

5 Ibid.

6 Philip Yenawine, *Visual Thinking Strategies: Using Art to Deepen Learning Across School Disciplines* (Cambridge, MA: Harvard Education Press, 2013), 25.

7 See David K. Dickinson and Miriam W. Smith, "Long-Term Effects of Preschool Teachers' Book Reading on Low-Income Children's Vocabulary and Story Comprehension," *Reading Research Quarterly* 29, no. 2 (1994): 105–19.

8 See Margaret G. McKeown and Isabel L. Beck, "Encouraging Young Children's Language Interactions with Stories," in *Handbook of Early Literacy Research*, Vol. 2, eds. David K. Dickinson and Susan B. Neuman (New York: Guilford, 2006), 281–94.

9 See Grover J. (Russ) Whitehurst, "Dialogic Reading: An Effective Way to Read to Preschoolers," http://www.readingrockets.org/article/400.

10 See Grover J. Whitehurst, David S. Arnold, Jeffery N. Epstein, Andrea L. Angell, Meagan Smith, and Janet E. Fischel, "A Picture Book Reading Intervention in Day Care and Home for Children from Low-Income Families," *Developmental Psychology* 30, no. 5, (Sept. 1994): 679–89; and Anne C. Hargrave and Monique Sénéchal, "A Book Reading Intervention with Preschool Children Who Have Limited Vocabularies: The Benefits of Regular and Dialogic Reading," *Early Childhood Research Quarterly* 15, no. 1 (2000): 75–90. Also see note 7 above.

11 Colleen E. Huebner and Andrew N. Meltzoff, "Intervention to Change Parent-Child Reading Style: A Comparison of Instructional Methods," *Journal of Applied Developmental Psychology* 26, no. 3 (May/June 2005): 296–313. See more at "Hear and Say Reading with Toddlers: Child Trends," last modified November 3, 2008, http://www.childtrends.org/?programs=hear-and-say-reading-with-toddlers.

12 Richard Macksey, foreword to *Paratexts: Thresholds of Interpretation*, by Gérard Genette, trans. Jane E. Lewin (New York: Cambridge University Press, 1997), xi. Originally published as *Seuils* (Paris, Éditions du Seuil, 1987).

Chapter 1 • That's About the Size of It

13 See Roger Sutton and Martha V. Parravano, *A Family of Readers: The Book Lover's Guide to Children's and Young Adult Literature* (Somerville, MA: Candlewick Press, 2010), 6.

14 Unsigned review of *Leonardo's Horse*, by Jean Fritz, illustrated by Hudson Talbott, *Publishers Weekly*, September 17, 2001, http://www.publishersweekly.com/978-0-399-23576-4.

15 See Leonard S. Marcus, "Carry On: 'The Further Tale of Peter Rabbit' and More," *New York Times*, November 9, 2012.

16 Sarah Ellis, review of *Open This Little Book*, by Jesse Klausmeier, *Horn Book Magazine* (Jan./Feb. 2014): 30.

17 Leonard S. Marcus, *Ways of Telling: Conversations on the Art of the Picture Book* (New York: Dutton Children's Books, 2002), 204–5.

Chapter 2 • Coming Attractions

18 See Nancy Gilson, "Words on Pictures: Critics Lament Lack of Children's Books with Illustrations That Whisper," *The Columbus Dispatch*, February 10, 2002.

19 See Leonard S. Marcus, "An Interview with Neal Porter," *Horn Book Magazine*, March/April 2014, http://www.hbook.com/2014/03/choosing-books/horn-book-magazine/interview-neal-porter/.

Chapter 4 • Slow Down and Look

20 "Laura Seeger talks about her picture book BULLY," Macmillan Children's Publishing Group video, 3:05. July 24, 2013, http://us.macmillan.com/bully/LauraSeeger.

21 Maria Nikolajeva and Carole Scott, *How Picturebooks Work* (New York: Routledge, 2006), 241, 256.

Chapter 5 • Knocked Out by Type

22 Kieran Slattery, in conversation with the author, July 27, 2013.

23 Frank Serafini and Jennifer Clausen, "Typography as Semiotic Resource," *Journal of Visual Literacy* 31, no. 2 (2012): 12-29.

24 David Wiesner, "2002 Caldecott Speech—David Wiesner's Caldecott Medal Acceptance Speech for *The Three Pigs*," accessed June 13, 2013, http://www.hmhbooks.com/wiesner/2002-speech-html.

25 Barbara Z. Kiefer, *The Potential of Picturebooks: From Visual Literacy to Aesthetic Understanding* (Englewood Cliffs, NJ: Merrill/Prentice Hall, 1995), 36.

26 Leonard S. Marcus, "Give 'Em Helvetica: Picture Book Type," *Horn Book Magazine*, (Sept./Oct. 2012): 40–45.

27 Jane Doonan, *Looking at Pictures in Picture Books* (Stroud, UK: Thimble Press, 1993), 9.

Notes

28 Frank Serafini and Jennifer Clausen, "Typography as Semiotic Resource," *Journal of Visual Literacy* 31, no. 2 (2012): 12–29.

29 Molly Bang, *Picture This: How Pictures Work* (San Francisco: Chronicle Books, 2000), 80. Originally published as *Picture This: Perception and Composition* (Boston: Little, Brown, 1991).

Chapter 6 • Gutter Talk and More

30 Barbara Bader, *American Picturebooks from Noah's Ark to the Beast Within* (New York: Macmillan, 1976), 1.

31 "A Letter from Brian Selznick," Amazon.com Exclusive, accessed August 13, 2013, http://www.amazon.com/Invention-Hugo-Cabret-Brian-Selznick/dp/0439813786.

Chapter 7 • "Children, Children, What Do You See?"

32 Chris Raschka, "32 Pages and a Chipmunk; Or, What Is Appropriate Art for Children?" *Book Links* 7, no. 4 (March 1998): 36.

33 L. S. Vygotsky, *Mind in Society*: *The Development of Higher Psychological Processes* (Cambridge, MA: Harvard University Press, 1978), 86.

34 Alison King, "From Sage on the Stage to Guide on the Side," *College Teaching* 41, no. 1 (1993): 30–35.

Chapter 8 • The Picture Book Playground

35 Philip Yenawine, *Visual Thinking Strategies: Using Art to Deepen Learning Across School Disciplines* (Cambridge, MA: Harvard Education Press, 2013), 154.

36 E. B. White, "Some Remarks on Humor," preface to *A Subtreasury of American Humor*, eds. E. B. White and K. S. White (New York: Coward-McCann, 1941), xvii.

37 See, for example, Louise Rosenblatt, "Efferent and Aesthetic Reading," chap. 3 in *The Reader, the Text, the Poem: A Transactional Theory of the Literary Work* (Carbondale: Southern Illinois University Press, 1978), or Hugh Walpole, *Reading: An Essay* (New York: Harper, 1927).

38 Arthur Krystal, "Kid Roberts and Me" in *Rereadings: Seventeen Writers Revisit Books They Love*, ed. Anne Fadiman (New York: Farrar Straus & Giroux, 2005), 69.

39 Wendy Lukehart, "Playgrounds for the Mind: Drawn to Delight: How Picturebooks Work (and Play) Today," *Children & Libraries* 8, no. 3 (Winter 2010): 32–35.

40 "Beyond the Secret Garden" (conference, California State University, Fresno, CA, April 25–27, 2003).

Conclusion • The Story Continues

41 Lolly Robinson, "What Do You See?: The Eric Carle Museum of Picture Book Art," *Horn Book Magazine*, May/June 2003, http://archive.hbook.com/magazine/articles/2003/may03_robinson.asp.

Resources • Leading Whole Book Storytimes

42 Ellin Oliver Keene and Susan Zimmermann, *Mosaic of Thought: The Power of Comprehension Strategy Instruction*: *Teaching Comprehension in a Reader's Workshop* (Portsmouth, NH: Heinemann, 2007).

43 Barbara Bader, *American Picturebooks from Noah's Ark to the Beast Within* (New York: Macmillan, 1976), 1.

Image Credits

Back flap

Official museum logo: "The Very Hungry Caterpillar" by Eric Carle. Copyright © 1969 & 1987 by Eric Carle. All rights reserved. Used with permission from the Eric Carle Studio. "Mice" image by Leo Lionni. Copyright © 1989 by the estate of Leo Lionni. Used by permission. "Wild Things" image by Maurice Sendak. Copyright © 1963 by Maurice Sendak, reuse of image in The Eric Carle Museum logo copyright © 2014 by Maurice Sendak Estate, used by permission of The Wylie Agency LLC.

Preface

p. viii: © 2003 by Paul Shoul.

Introduction

p. xiii: © Simmons College. **p. xxi:** © Corey Feltovic.

Chapter 1

p. 2: From *Madeline* by Ludwig Bemelmans, copyright © 1939 by Ludwig Bemelmans, renewed © 1967 by Madeleine Bemelmans and Barbara Bemelmans Marciano. Used with permission of Viking Penguin, a division of Penguin Group (USA) LLC. **p. 5:** From *Blackout* by John Rocco. Jacket illustration copyright © 2011 by John Rocco. Reprinted by permission of Disney • Hyperion Books, an imprint of Disney Book Group, LLC. All rights reserved. **p. 6 (top):** From *The Very Hungry Caterpillar* by Eric Carle, copyright © 1969 and 1987 by Eric Carle. Used by permission of Philomel Books, a division of Penguin Group (USA) LLC. **p. 6 (bottom):** From *The Polar Express* by Chris Van Allsburg. Copyright © 1985 by Chris Van Allsburg. Reprinted by permission of Houghton Mifflin Harcourt Publishing Company. All rights reserved. **p. 7:** From *Georgia in Hawaii: When Georgia O'Keeffe Painted What She Pleased* by Amy Novesky. Jacket illustrations copyright © 2012 by Yuyi Morales. Reprinted by permission of Harcourt Children's Books, an imprint of Houghton Mifflin Harcourt Publishing Company. All rights reserved. **p. 8 (top):** From *Moses: When Harriet Tubman Led Her People to Freedom* by Carole Boston Weatherford. Jacket illustration copyright © 2006 by Kadir Nelson. Reprinted by permission of Disney • Hyperion Books, an imprint of Disney Book Group, LLC. All rights reserved. **p. 8 (bottom):** From *The Mountain That Loved a Bird* by Alice McLerran, illustrated by Eric Carle. Illustrations copyright © 1985 Eric Carle. Reprinted with the permission of Simon & Schuster Books for Young Readers, an imprint of Simon & Schuster Children's Publishing Division. **p. 9 (top):** From *Bringing the Rain to Kapiti Plain* by Verna Aardema, illustrated by Beatriz Vidal, copyright © 1981 by Beatriz Vidal, illustrations. Used with permission of Dial Books for Young Readers, a division of Penguin Group, (USA) LLC. **p. 9 (bottom):** From *Leonardo's Horse* by Jean Fritz, illustrated by Hudson Talbott, copyright © 2001 by Hudson Talbott, illustrations. Used by permission of G.P. Putnam's Sons, a division of Penguin Group (USA) LLC. **p. 10 (left):** From *Perfect Square* by Michael Hall. Copyright © 2011 by Michael Hall. Used by permission of HarperCollins Publishers. **p. 10 (right):** From *First the Egg* © 1999 by Laura Vaccaro Seeger. Used by permission of Roaring Brook Press. All rights reserved.

Chapter 2

p. 17 (jacket and spine): From *City Dog, Country Frog* by Mo Willems. Jacket illustration copyright © 2010 by Jon J Muth. Reprinted by permission of Disney • Hyperion Books, an imprint of Disney Book Group, LLC. All rights reserved. **p. 19 (front and back):** From *Grandfather's Journey* by Allen Say. Copyright © 1993 by Allen Say. Reprinted by permission of Houghton Mifflin Harcourt Publishing Company. All rights reserved. **p. 22:** From *Grandfather's Journey* by Allen Say. Copyright © 1993 by Allen Say. Reprinted by permission of Houghton Mifflin Harcourt Publishing Company. All rights reserved.

Chapter 3

p. 26: From *Brown Bear, Brown Bear, What Do You See?* © 1983 by Bill Martin Jr. Illustrations © 1983 by Eric Carle. Reprinted by permission of Henry Holt Books for Young Readers. All rights reserved. **p. 30 (both images):** From *Hush Little Baby: A Folk Song with Pictures* by Marla Frazee. Copyright © 1997 by Marla Frazee. Reprinted by permission of Harcourt Children's Books, an imprint of Houghton Mifflin Harcourt Publishing Company. All rights reserved.

Chapter 4

p. 32 (top): From *Little Red Riding Hood* by Trina Schart Hyman. Copyright © 1987 by Trina Schart Hyman. Used by permission of Holiday House, Inc. **p. 32 (bottom):** From *Hush Little Baby: A Folk Song with Pictures* by Marla Frazee. Copyright © 1997 by Marla Frazee. Reprinted by permission of Harcourt Children's Books, an imprint of Houghton Mifflin Harcourt Publishing Company. All rights reserved. **p. 33 (both images):** From *Hush Little Baby: A Folk Song with Pictures* by Marla Frazee. Copyright © 1997 by Marla Frazee. Reprinted by permission of Harcourt Children's Books, an imprint of Houghton Mifflin Harcourt Publishing Company. All rights reserved. **p. 35:** From *Bully* © 2013 by Laura Vaccaro Seeger. Used by permission of Roaring Brook Press. All rights reserved. **p. 36:** From *The Very Hungry Caterpillar* by Eric Carle, copyright © 1969 and 1987 by Eric Carle. Used by permission of Philomel Books, a division of Penguin Group (USA) LLC.

Chapter 5

p. 39: From *What's Your Sound, Hound the Hound?* by Mo Willems. Copyright © 2010 by Mo Willems. Used by permission of HarperCollins Publishers. **p. 42 (top):** From *Little Pig Joins the Band* © 2011 by David Hyde Costello, Charlesbridge Publishing. **p. 42 (bottom):** From *A Crow of His Own* © 2015 by Megan Dowd Lambert, illustrations © 2015 by David Hyde Costello, Charlesbridge Publishing. **p. 44:** From *Bully* © 2013 by Laura Vaccaro Seeger. Used by permission of Roaring Brook Press. All rights reserved. **p. 45:** From *A Visitor for Bear*. Text copyright © 2008 by Bonny Becker. Illustrations copyright © 2008 by Kady MacDonald Denton. Reproduced by permission of the publisher, Candlewick Press, Somerville, MA. **p. 48 (top):** From *The Sleeping Beauty* by Trina Schart Hyman. Copyright © 1977 by Trina Schart Hyman. Used by permission of Little, Brown and Company. All rights reserved. **p. 48: (bottom)** From *Goldilocks and the Three Bears* by James Marshall, copyright © 1988 by James Marshall. Used by permission of Dial Books for Young Readers, a division of Penguin Group (USA) LLC.

Chapter 6

p. 53: From *When Marian Sang*, text by Pam Muñoz Ryan, illustrations by Brian Selznick © 2002 Brian Selznick. Used with permission of the illustrator. **p. 56:** From *Brown Bear, Brown Bear, What Do You See?* © 1983 by Bill Martin Jr. Illustrations © 1983 by Eric Carle. Reprinted by permission of Henry Holt Books for Young Readers. All rights reserved.

Image Credits

p. 59: From *Hush Little Baby: A Folk Song with Pictures* by Marla Frazee. Copyright ☺ 1997 by Marla Frazee. Reprinted by permission of Harcourt Children's Books, an imprint of Houghton Mifflin Harcourt Publishing Company. All rights reserved. **p. 60 (all three images):** From *Yo! Yes?* by Chris Raschka. Scholastic Inc./Orchard Books. Copyright © 1993 by Chris Raschka. Used by permission. **p. 61:** From *Journey*. Copyright © 2013 by Aaron Becker. Reproduced by permission of the publisher, Candlewick Press, Somerville, MA. **p. 62:** From *Journey*. Copyright © 2013 by Aaron Becker. Reproduced by permission of the publisher, Candlewick Press, Somerville, MA. **p. 65:** © Megan Dowd Lambert, courtesy of the author.

Chapter 7
p. 70: From *10 Little Rubber Ducks* by Eric Carle. Copyright © 2005 by Eric Carle. Used by permission of HarperCollins Publishers. **p. 75:** From *Millions of Cats* by Wanda Gág, © 1928 by Wanda Gág, renewed © 1956 by Robert Janssen. Used by permission of Coward-McCann, Inc., a division of Penguin Group (USA) LLC. **p. 76:** From *The Snowy Day* by Ezra Jack Keats, copyright © 1962 by Ezra Jack Keats, renewed © 1990 by Martin Pope, executor. Used by permission of Viking Penguin, a division of Penguin Group (USA) LLC. **p. 77:** From *Come Along, Daisy!* by Jane Simmons. Copyright © 2001 by Jane Simmons. Used by permission of Little, Brown and Company. All rights reserved. **p. 78:** From *Come Along, Daisy!* by Jane Simmons. Copyright © 2001 by Jane Simmons. Used by permission of Little, Brown and Company. All rights reserved. **p. 79:** From *Knuffle Bunny: A Cautionary Tale* by Mo Willems. Illustrations copyright © 2004 by Mo Willems. Reprinted by permission of Disney • Hyperion Books, an imprint of Disney Book Group, LLC. All rights reserved.

Chapter 8
p. 87: From *The Very Busy Spider* by Eric Carle, copyright © 1984 by Eric Carle Corporation. Used by permission of Philomel Books, a division of Penguin Group (USA) LLC. **p. 92 (top):** From *Extra Yarn* by Mac Barnett. Illustrations copyright © 2012 by Jon Klassen. Used by permission of HarperCollins Publishers. **p. 92 (bottom):** From *I Want My Hat Back*. Copyright © 2011 by John Klassen. Reproduced by permission of the publisher, Candlewick Press, Somerville, MA. **p. 93 (top):** From *And Then It's Spring* © 1999 by Julie Fogliano. Illustrations © 1999 by Erin E. Stead. Reprinted by permission of Roaring Brook Press. All rights reserved. **p. 93 (bottom left):** From *And Then It's Spring* © 1999 by Julie Fogliano. Illustrations © 1999 by Erin E. Stead. Reprinted by permission of Roaring Brook Press. All rights reserved. **p. 93 (bottom right):** From *A Sick Day for Amos McGee* © 1999 by Phillip C. Stead. Illustrations © 1999 by Erin E. Stead. Reprinted by permission of Roaring Brook Press. All rights reserved.

Conclusion
p. 97: © 2014 by Jim Gipe. **p. 98:** From *Pete the Cat and His Four Groovy Buttons* by Eric Litwin. Copyright © 2012 by James Dean. Used by permission of HarperCollins Publishers.

Index

10 Little Rubber Ducks (Carle), 69–70, *70*

Aardema, Verna, 8
aberrant readings
   continuous narrative, 72–76
   defined, 129
   illusion of movement, 79–80
   perspectives of art, 77–78
   sample questions, 125–126
aesthetic reading, 83–84
Agoglia, Rosemary, 20, 113–114
air frames, 60, 61, 62–63, 100, 101, 109, 129
American Library Association, 22, 44
And Then It's Spring (Fogliano & Stead), 92, *93*, 94
Anderson, Marian, 53
architectural plan, xv–xvi, xx, xxiii, 15, 122
Arnheim, Rudolf, 71
Association for Library Service to Children, xx, 84–85
At Night (Bean), 11

Bader, Barbara, 51, 52, 112
Bang, Molly, xiv, 10, 50, 110
Barnett, Mac, 91
Bean, Jonathan, 11
Becker, Aaron, 61–62, *61*, *62*
Becker, Bonnie, 45–46
Bemelmans, Ludwig, vi, *2*, 3–4
Benson, Patrick, 54
bindings, 22, 52, 54, 59, 129
Blackout (Rocco), 5, *5*
blind stamp, 21, 22, 23, 121, 129
Book Links, 71
Boston Globe-Horn Book Award Committee, xi, 91
Boston Globe-Horn Book (honors and awards), 12, 92

Boyd, Brian, 85–86
Bringing the Rain to Kapiti Plain (Aardema & Vidal), 8, *9*
Brown Bear, Brown Bear, What Do You See? (Martin Jr. & Carle), 25, 26–28, *26*, 50, 55–58, *56*, 61, 66, 70–71, 99
Bully (Seeger), 34–35, *35*, 44, *44*

Caldecott awards, 40–41, 47, 54, 61–62, 64, 93
Caldecott committee, 64, 96
the Carle. *see* Eric Carle Museum of Picture Book Art
Carle, Barbara, vii
Carle, Eric, vii, 6, *6*, 8, *8*, 25, 26, 27, 28, 35, 36, *36*, 55, *56*, 57, 58, 61, 69, 87, *87*, 88, 99
Carrot Seed, The, (Krauss & Johnson), 92
casing, 20–23, 121, 129
Chambers, Aidan, xi–xii
City Dog, Country Frog (Willems & Muth), 16–17, *17*, 25
Clark, H. Nichols B. "Nick," xiv, xvii–xviii
Clausen, Jennifer, 40, 49
Clever Jack Takes the Cake (Fleming & Karas), 28
clothbound casings, 20–23, 29, 121, 129
co-constructive approach, vii–viii, xii, xix–xx, 117, 124, 129
codex, x, xi, 95, 96, 128, 129
Collier, Brian, 64
Come Along, Daisy! (Simmons), 77–78, *77*, *78*
coming attractions. *see* jackets and covers
continuous narrative, 52–53, 54, 74–75, *75*, 76–77, *76*, 132
copyright page, 98, *98*, 129–130
Costello, David Hyde, 41–42, *42*

Index

cover board, 21, 130
Crane, Walter, xv–xvii, xx, xxiii, 15, 122
critical reading, 83–84
Crow of His Own, A, (Lambert & Costello), 42, *42*

Darwin, Charles, 85
Dave the Potter: Artist, Poet, Slave (Hill & Collier), 64–65
Dean, James, 98, *98*
dedication page, 33, 35, 123, 130
Denton, Kady MacDonald, 45, *45*
dialogic reading, xx, xxi, 130
digital age, xx–xxi, 95–96
Doonan, Jane, xiv, 49
dopamine, 85
double-page spread, 10, 52–55, 58–59, 62, 67, 74–77, 89, 101, 130
"drama of the turning of the page," 51, 52, 112
dual-image jackets, 17–19, 120

ebooks, x–xi, 95
ecstatic reading, 83–84, 101–102
Ella Fitzgerald: The Tale of a Vocal Virtuosa (Pinkney & Pinkney), 7
Ellis, Sarah, xi, 12
endpapers, 25–30
    as visual overture, 25–27, 29–30
    defined, 130
    important motif or object introduced, 29
    in *Brown Bear,* 25, 26–28, *26,* 66, 70–71
    in *Hush, Little Baby,* 29–30, *30*
    in *Very Hungry Caterpillar,* 35–36, *36*
    link to book content, child observations, 26–28, 35–36
    paratexts, 37
    sample questions, 121–122
    single-color, 29–30, *30,* 31, 122
    visual backstory, 28, 67, 122
Eric Carle Museum of Picture Book Art, vii–viii, *viii,* ix, xvii–xviii, xix, 5, 12, 20, 25, 69, 74, 79, 89, 97, 99, 100, 113
Every Child Ready to Read, xx
Extra Yarn (Barnett & Klassen), 91–92, *92*

facing pages, 51, 52, 60, 67, 75–76, 130
Fadiman, Anne, 83
Family of Readers, A, (Sutton & Parravano, eds.), 4–5

First the Egg (Seeger), 10, *10*
Fleming, Candace, 28
Fogliano, Julie, 21, 22, 29, 92, 93
foil stamp, 21, 22, *22,* 23, 121, 130
framed art, 57–58, 61, 62–64, 65, 101, 124, 125
Frazee, Marla, 29–30, *30,* 31, 32, *32,* 33, *33,* 34, 58–59, *58*
Frederick (Lionni), 66–69
Fritz, Jean, 9
front matter, 31–37
    children's observations of, inviting, 35–36, 37, 109, 122
    defined, 130
    Frazee's *Hush, Little Baby,* 31–34, *32, 33,* 58–59, *59*
    importance of, 34–37
    paratexts, 36–37
    sample questions, 122–123
    title pages, *33,* 37, 58–59, *59,* 132
frontispiece, xvi, 32, *32,* 34–35, 130
full-bleed art, 10, 32, 34–35, 47, 54, 55–57, 61–62, 63, 64–65, 101, 124, 130

Gág, Wanda, 7, 74, 75, *75*
Genette, Gérard, xxii–xxiii, 132
Georgia in Hawaii (Novesky & Morales), 7, *7*
Goldilocks and the Three Bears (Marshall), 47–48, *48*
Grandfather's Journey (Say), 17–19, *19,* 22–23, *22,* 25, 120
Gravett, Emily, 16
Grey Lady and the Strawberry Snatcher, The, (Bang), 10–11
gutters
    and bindings, 54, 58, 129
    and loss of picture space, 54–55, 125
    defined, 131
    double-page spreads and, 52–55, 58–59
    full-bleed art and, 10
    incorporating into story, 51, 58–60
    sample questions, 109, 125

half-title page, 32, 131
Hall, Michael, 9–10, *10*
Hawkes, Kevin, 7, 45–46
Henkes, Kevin, 29
Hill, Laban Carrick, 64
Hillenbrand, Will, 15

Horn Book at Simmons Colloquium, xi
Horn Book Magazine, 46, 99–100
Housen, Abigail, xviii–xix
How Picturebooks Work (Nikolajeva & Scott), 36–37
humor, dissecting, 83
Hush, Little Baby (Frazee), 29–30, *30*, 31–34, *32, 33*, 58–59, *59*
Hyman, Trina Schart, 32, *32*, 47, *48*

"I have a dog" statements, 110–111, 127
I Want My Hat Back (Klassen), 91, 92, *92*
If You Want to See a Whale (Fogliano & Stead), 21–22, 29
illusion of movement, 79–80
ink stamp, 23, 121, 131
inquiry-based approach to art, xix, 20, 81
interactive experience, vii–viii, xx, 69, 94, 96, 99, 129
intertextual reading, 45, 87–94, 128, 129
intraiconic text, 16, 42, 47, *48*, 131
Invention of Hugo Cabret, The, (Selznick), 54

Jack and the Beanstalk (Kellogg), 28
jackets and covers, 15–24
    as "coming attraction" poster, 15, 26, 41
    children engaged by, 20, 23–24, 67
    clothbound casings, 20–23, 29, 121, 129
    definition, 129, 131
    dual-images, 17–19, 22–23, 119–120
    embellished boards, 23–24, 121
    paratexts, 37, 124
    sample questions, 119–121
    typography of, 41
    wraparound designs, 16–17, 120
John Henry (Lester & Pinkney), 7, 57
Johnson, Crockett, 92
Journey (Becker), 61–62, *61, 62*

Karas, G. Brian, 28
Keats, Ezra Jack, 76, *76*
Keene, Ellin Oliver, 111
Kellogg, Steven, 7, 28
"kids say the darndest things," xxii, 5, 6, 12, 17, 18, 19, 23, 27–28, 36, 38–39, 41, 42, 43, 45, 56, 57, 59, 64, 66–67, 68–69, 71, 75, 89, 90, 91–92, 93, 101
Kiefer, Barbara Z., 41
King, Alison, 74
King, Carole, 90

Klassen, Jon, 91, 92, *92*
Klausmeier, Jesse, 12
knockout type, 50, 131
Knudsen, Michelle, 45–46
Knuffle Bunny: A Cautionary Tale (Willems), 79, *79*
Krauss, Ruth, 92
Krystal, Arthur, 83–84

Lambert, Megan Dowd, v, *xxi*, 42, 99–100
Lambert-Mergendahl, Caroline, 12, 17, 39, 41–42, 91–94
Lambert-Mergendahl, Emilia, 64, 77–78, 87–89, 91
Lambert-Mergendahl, Natayja, 3
Lambert-Mergendahl, Stevie, *xxi*, 3, 64–65, *65*, 91
Lambert-Wright, Rory, xvii
landscape orientation, 4, 6–7, 8, 118, 131
layout. *see* page design
Leading Whole Book Approach Storytimes, 108–14
    beginning, 108–109
    collective shushing, 112–113
    keeping kids on topic, 110–111
    losing the story, concerns, 114–115
    moving the story along, 111–113
    quiet groups, handling, 109–110
    talkers and listeners, 113–114, 127
learning to read, 20, 38–40, 71, 80
Lee, Suzy, 12
Leonardo's Horse (Fritz & Talbott), 9, *9*
Lester, Julius, 7, 57
Library Lion (Knudsen & Hawkes), 45–46
Lies, Brian, 76
Lion & the Mouse, The, (Pinkney), 47
Lionni, Leo, 66, 67
listeners vs. talkers, 113–114, 127
Little Pig Joins the Band (Costello), 41, *42*
Little Red Riding Hood (Hyman), 32, *32*
Litwin, Eric, 98
loose-back Smyth-sewn binding, 54, 131
Lukehart, Wendy, 84–86

Macksey, Richard, xxii–xxiii
Macmillan, 22
Madeline (Bemelmans), vi, *2*, 3–4, 5, 6, 11, 13, 25, 96
Magic School Bus, 74
Magritte, René, 43

Index

Marcus, Leonard S., 13, 21, 46

Markus, Anna, 3

Marshall, James, 47–48, *48*

Martin Jr., Bill, 25, 57, 99

Mass Literacy, ix

metafictive work, 12, 32, 131

metatextual content, 131

Millions of Cats (Gág), 7, 74–75, *75*

Milne, A. A., 88

Mind in Society: The Development of Higher Psychological Processes (Vygotsky), 73

misreadings of text. *see* aberrant readings

Mole and the Baby Bird (Newman & Benson), 54

Monaco, James, xi

Morales, Yuri, 7

More (Springman & Lies), 76–77

Moses: When Harriet Tubman Led Her People to Freedom (Weatherford & Nelson), 7, *8*

Mountain That Loved a Bird, The, (McLerran & Carle), 8, *8*

multimodal texts, x, xv, xxiii, 131

Muth, Jon J., 16–17, *17*

Myers, Chris, 5–6

Myth, Magic, and Mystery (Hearn, Clark & Clark), xiv, xvii

Neal Porter Books, 22

negative space, 61, 131

Nelson, Kadir, 7, *8*

New York Times, 96

Newman, Marjorie, 54

Nikolajeva, Maria, 36–37

nonverbal expression, 58, 109–110

Novesky, Amy, 7

nurturing visual intelligence, 66–80. *see also* aberrant readings

    insights on *Frederick*, 66–69

    literacy skills developed, 71–72, 89

    perspectives of art, 77–78

    reading pictures, 18, 71, 78, 80, 100, 125

    representative/abstract art, 70

    sample questions, 125–127

    simultaneous succession, 74–77, 132

Nutshell Library (Sendak), 90

Of the Decorative Illustration of Books Old and New (Crane), xv–xvi

O'Keeffe, Georgia, 7

On the Origin of Stories (Boyd), 85–86

One Boy (Seeger), 10

"one-two-three" page turns, 112, 127

Open This Little Book (Klausmeier & Lee), 12

pacing, 51, 52, 60, 63, 99, 112

page design, 51–65

    air frames/white space, 60, 61, 62–63, 100, 101, 109, 129

    and story content, 58–60, 67

    bindings, 22, 52, 54, 58, 129

    double-page spread, 52–55, 58–59, 62, 67, 74–77, 89, 101, 130, 132

    framed art, 57–58, 61, 62–64, 65, 101, 124, 125

    full-bleed art, 10, 32, 34–35, 47, 54, 55–57, 61–62, 63, 64–65, 101, 124, 130

    gutters. *see* gutters

    impact on reading experience, 51

    negative space, 61, 131

    pacing, 51, 52, 60, 63, 99

    sample questions, 124–125

    shared reading experiences, 4–5, 66, 96–98, 109

    whole book approach, 51, 52, 55

page opening, 10, 52, 131

paratexts, xxii, 28, 30, 36–37, 66, 67, 84, 94, 124, 132

Paratexts: Thresholds of Interpretation (Genette), xxii–xxiii

Parravano, Martha V., 4–5

Paul Bunyan (Kellogg), 7

peer collaboration, 73

PEER sequence of reading, xx, 130

Perfect Square (Hall), 9–10, *10*

perspectives of art, 77–78

Pete the Cat and His Four Groovy Buttons (Litwin & Dean), 97–98, *98*

picture book playground, 81–94. *see also* nurturing visual intelligence

    "cognitive playground," 85–86

    "ecstatic criticism" and play, 84–85, 86–87, 127–128

    intertextual connections, and artist styles, 87–94, 129

    progressive education, 20, 81–82

    sample questions, 128

    whole book approach, 86, 94, 96

picture books
    architectural plan, xv–xvii, xx, xxiii, 15, 122
    as sequential art form, 75–76
    as "theater of the lap," 15
    as visual art form, xiii–xv, xxi, 51, 84, 114, 127–128
    biographies, 7
    emotional connection to, 63–65
    focus on visual component, xx–xxi
    graduate course study of, xiii–xvi, xvii, xxi
    in the digital age, x–xi, 95–96
    lifelong attachment to, 22
    reading vs. finishing, 78, 111
    thematic storytime, xviii, xxi–xxii
    "thinginess" or "bookness," v, xi, 96–97
    visual literacy skills, 71–72, 89
"Picture Books No Longer a Staple for Children" (*New York Times*), 96
picture plane, 54, 57, 61, 74, 132
Pinkney, Brian, 7
Pinkney, Jerry, 7, 47, 57
playfulness, and art, 84–86, 127–128
Polar Express, The, 6, 6, 23–24
Porter, Neal, 21
portrait orientation, 4, 5–6, 7–8, 12, 118, 132
Potter, Beatrix, 11, 12
Prabhaker, Emily, 97–98, 97
Prabhaker, Lucy, 98
progressive education, 20, 81–82
Public Library Association, xx
Publishers Weekly, 9
Puffin Books, 8

quiet groups, 109–110, 113–114

raised textures, 87–88
Raschka, Chris, v–vi, 49, 59–60, 60, 71–72, 109
reader-response theory, 72–73, 110–111
reading aloud. *see* typography
"reading pictures," 18, 71, 78, 80, 100, 125. *see also* nurturing visual intelligence
Reading Rainbow, 8
Really Rosie CD, 90–91
recto page, 10, 32, 33, 51, 52, 58, 60, 63, 74, 76, 101, 132
Rereadings: Seventeen Writers Revisit Books They Love (Fadiman), 83–84

Robinson, Lolly, 99–100
Ryan, Pam Muñoz, 53

sans serif, 46, 132
Say, Allen, 17–18, 19, *19*, 22, *22*, 23, 120
schema, 73, 111
Scieszka, Jon, 46
Scott, Carole, 37
Seeger, Laura Vaccaro, 9, 10, *10*, 34–35, *35*, 44, *44*
Selznick, Brian, 53, *53*, 54
Sendak, Maurice, 62–63, 89, 90
Serafini, Frank, 40, 49
serif, 132
shaped formats, 8–9, 132
Shepard, Ernest H., 88
shushing, 112–113
Sick Day for Amos McGee, A, (Stead & Stead), 93, *93*, 94
Simmons, Jane, 77, *77*, 78, *78*
Simmons College, vii, viii, xiii, *xiii*, xxi, 97
simultaneous succession, 74–77, 132
Sleeping Beauty, The, (Hyman), 47, *48*
Smith, Lane, 46
Smith College, 3
Snowy Day, The, (Keats), 76, *76*
spine, 16, 17, 132
Springman, I. C., 76
square trim, 9–11, 118
Stead, Erin, 21, 22, 29, 92, 93, *93*, 94
Stead, Philip C., 93
Stinky Cheese Man and Other Fairly Stupid Tales, The, (Scieszka & Smith), 46, 47
surrealist art, 43
Swamp Angel (Isaacs & Zelinsky), 7

Talbott, Hudson, 9, *9*
Tale of Peter Rabbit, The, (Potter), 12
talkers and listeners, handling, 113–114, 127
textured images, 87–88
"theater of the lap," 15
Thinker, The, (Rodin), 89
Three Pigs, The, (Wiesner), 40–41
Thwaite, Ann, 88, 89
title pages, xvi, 32, 34–35, 36, 37, 58–59, 60, 121, 132
trim size and orientation, 3–14
    adult-child shared reading experience, 4–5, 66, 96–98, 109
    children's observations of, 11–12

Index

definitions, 133

landscape orientation, 4, 6–7, 8, 118, 131

large and little books, 11–14, 118–119

portrait orientation, 4, 5–6, 7–8, 118, 132

reprints and redesigns, flaws, 8, *9*, 12–13

sample questions, 118–119

shaped formats, 8–9, 132

square layout, 9–11, 118

varying, 12

Tubman, Harriet, 64

typeface, 40, 41, 43, 123, 133

typography, 37–50

children's observations of, 41–42

contrast, in visual art, 50

early literacy, 38–40, 49–50

engaging children with, 43–44, 45–47

in *The Three Pigs* (Wiesner), 40–41

integrative, responses to, 48–49

intraiconic text, 16, 42, 47, 129

lettering, 67

on jackets and covers, 41

onomatopoeic sounds, 47

reading aloud, effect on, 44–46, 49, 123

sample questions, 123–124

seamless integration into visual layout, 47–50, *48*, 124

tone conveyed, 40, 123

varying by character, 43

visual elements of speech, 38, 40

"Typography as Semiotic Resource" (Serafini & Clausen), 49

Van Allsburg, Chris, 6, *6*, 23–24

verso pages, 10, 11, 32, 34, 51, 52, 59, 60, 63, 74, 76, 101, 125, 133

Very Busy Spider, The, (Carle), xviii, 87–88, *87*

Very Hungry Caterpillar, The, (Carle), vi, 6, *6*, 35–36, *36*, 58

Very Quiet Cricket, The, (Carle), 88

Vidal, Beatriz, 8, *9*

vignette, 33, 98, 133

Visitor for Bear, A, (Becker & Denton), 45–46, *45*, 47

Visual Thinking Strategies: Using Art to Deepen Learning Across School Disciplines (Yenawine), 82

Visual Thinking Strategies (VTS), xix, 18, 70, 73–74, 82, 110, 113–114, 120, 122–123, 126–127, 133

Voices in the Park (Browne), 43

Vygotsky, L. S., 73

Weatherford, Carole Boston, 7

Wells, Rosemary, 13

Wemberly Worried (Henkes), 29

What's Your Sound, Hound the Hound (Willems), 38–39, *39*

When Marian Sang (Ryan & Selznick), 53, *53*

When Sophie Gets Angry—Really, Really Angry (Bang), 110

Where the Wild Things Are (Sendak), 62–63, 89–90, 100, 109

White, E. B., 83

white space, 60, 61, 62–63, 101, 109, 129

Whitehurst, Grover J. "Russ," xix–xx, 130

Whole Book Approach. *see also* Visual Thinking Strategies (VTS)

as "ecstatic criticism," 101–102

as inquiry-based approach to art, xiv, 20, 81

book production, 59, 99

book size and layout, 4, 5, 6

collaborative experience, 73, 75–76, 126–127

"conducting an orchestra," 100

development of, vii–xxiii, 82

"ecstatic criticism" and play, 83–84

front-matter pages, 35–36, 37

graduate course and training, 97

learning skills developed, 100–101

looking at entirety of jacket (cover), 16–18, 23–24

nonverbal, physical expressions, 58, 110

open-ended questions, xix, xx, 18, 26, 70, 73–74, 110, 114

opportunity to respond to art, 65, 66, 71, 84, 98–99

page design, 51, 52, 55

participants vs. spectators, 101–102

resistance to, by adults, 83

Sample Questions

endpapers, 121–122

front matter, 122–123

jackets and covers, 119–121

nurturing visual intelligence, 125–127

overview, 116

page design, 124–125

trim size and orientation, 118–119

    typography, 123–124
    visual thinking, 117, 118
shared reading experience, x, 4–5, 20, 22,
    72, 92, 96–98, 109
single-color endpapers, 29–30, *30*, 31
slowing down pace of reading, 84, 94
sophistication of children's insights, xxii,
    66–67, 68–69, 93–94
"stopping and starting" concerns, 83, 100,
    114–115, 127
Wiesner, David, 24, 40–41
Willems, Mo, 16–17, 38–39, *39*, 79, *79*
Wings (Myers), 5–6
Wolf Won't Bite! (Gravett), 16
wordless pictures, 10, 32, 33, 40, 47, 53, 54,
    63, 89, 133
wraparound art, 16–17, 18, 120

Yenawine, Philip, xix, 82, 133
Yo! Yes? (Raschka), 49, 60, *60*, 61, 109

Zimmerman, Susan, 111